P9-BYR-020

NATIONAL GEOGRAPHIC DIRECTIONS

ALSO BY JOHN EDGAR WIDEMAN

A Glance Away
Hurry Home
The Lynchers
Damballah
Hiding Place
Sent for You Yesterday
Brothers and Keepers
Reuben
Fever: Twelve Stories
Philadelphia Fire
All Stories Are True
Fatheralong
The Cattle Killing
Two Cities
Hoop Roots

The Island

JOHN EDGAR WIDEMAN

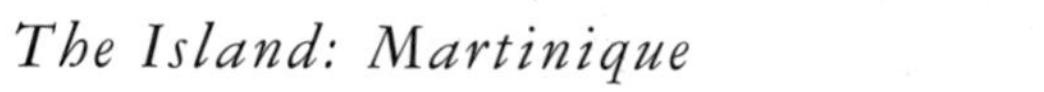

The Island: Martinique

NATIONAL GEOGRAPHIC DIRECTIONS

NATIONAL GEOGRAPHIC
Washington D.C.

Published by the National Geographic Society
1145 17th Street, N.W., Washington, D.C. 20036-4688

Library of Congress Cataloging-in-Publication Data

Wideman, John Edgar
The island, Martinique / [John Edgar Wideman].
p. cm. -- (National Geographic directions)
ISBN 0-7922-6533-5 (hc.)
1. Martinique--Description and travel. 2. Wideman, John Edgar--Journeys--Martinique.
I. Title. II. Series.

F2081.2 .W53 2003
917.298'2--dc21

2002037962

One of the world's largest nonprofit scientific and educational organizations, the National Geographic Society was founded in 1888 "for the increase and diffusion of geographic knowledge." Fulfilling this mission, the Society educates and inspires millions every day through its magazines, books, television programs, videos, maps and atlases, research grants, the National Geographic Bee, teacher workshops, and innovative classroom materials. The Society is supported through membership dues, charitable gifts, and income from the sale of its educational products. This support is vital to National Geographic's mission to increase global understanding and promote conservation of our planet through exploration, research, and education. For more information, please call 1-800-NGS LINE (647-5463), write to the Society at the above address, or visit the Society's Web site at www.nationalgeographic.com.

Interior design by Michael Ian Kaye and Tuan Ching, Ogilvy & Mather, Brand Integration Group

Printed in the U.S.A.

To Frantz Fanon

CONTENTS

The Island

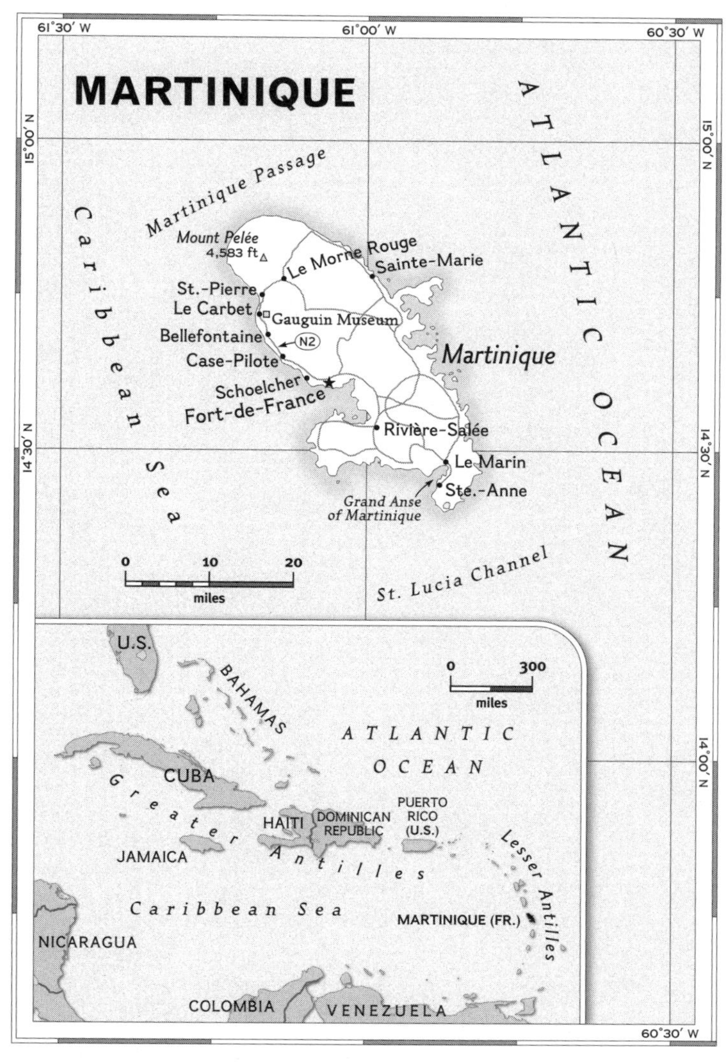
MARTINIQUE
61°30′ W
61°00′ W
60°30′ W
15°00′ N
14°30′ N
14°00′ N
ATLANTIC OCEAN
Martinique Passage
Caribbean Sea
Mount Pelée
4,583 ft
Le Morne Rouge
Sainte-Marie
St.-Pierre
Le Carbet
Gauguin Museum
Bellefontaine
N2
Case-Pilote
Martinique
Schoelcher
Fort-de-France
Rivière-Salée
Le Marin
Ste.-Anne
Grand Anse of Martinique
0
10
20
miles
St. Lucia Channel
U.S.
BAHAMAS
0
300
miles
ATLANTIC OCEAN
CUBA
Greater Antilles
HAITI
DOMINICAN REPUBLIC
PUERTO RICO (U.S.)
JAMAICA
Lesser Antilles
Caribbean Sea
MARTINIQUE (FR.)
NICARAGUA
COLOMBIA
VENEZUELA

A Chronology of the Island

4000 B.C.	Stone Age civilizations
1502	Columbus sights Martinique
1635	Belain d'Estambuc lands on Martinique, raises French flag. Extermination of indigenous peoples begins
1638	French build Fort Royal to secure colony
1640	Louis XIII authorizes importation of African slaves
1660	Population 2,642 slaves, 2,489 French*
1684	Population 10,656 slaves, 4,857 French
1685	Code Noir (a decree to regulate slavery) issued by Louis XIV
1714-1715	26,900 slaves on Martinique
1763	France's loss of Canada stimulates emigration/ development of West Indian possessions

1784	Republican Party abolishes slavery
1789	54,000 whites, 36,000 free people of color, 675,000 slaves in French West Indies
1789-1793	Revolution in France
1789-1796	British invade, occupy Martinique
1802	Napoleon recovers Martinique for France, rescinds abolition
1848	Slavery ends on Martinique
1858	Indentured laborers from India are imported
1900	Population 187,692
1902	City of St.-Pierre destroyed by eruption of Mount Pelée; 30,000 dead
1940-1943	France's Vichy (collaborationist) government rules Martinique
1941-1945	*Tropiques* magazine published. René Menil and Aimé and Suzanne Césaire inspire and edit this publication examining Martinique's culture from the point of view of African-descended people
1946	Martinique becomes a French *département,* or *région outre-mer*

* This statistic and many of those that follow are from Robin Blackburn's *Making of New World Slavery.*

INTRODUCTION

Introduction

Here I am on the brink of returning to Martinique, still trying to make sense of my first and only trip to the island. *"Le Pays des Revenants,"* as it was baptized by French priest Père Du Tertre—"the country of comers-back."

"The way of life in the country is so pleasant," wrote Du Tertre, "the temperature so good, and one lives there in such a state of straightforward freedom that I have never met one single man, nor one single woman, of all those who came back therefrom, in whom I have not remarked a most passionate desire to return thereunto." So yes, just as the good father predicted three centuries ago, I've often dreamed of returning to Martinique, especially on gray, blustery, bone-chilling winter days on this island of Manhattan, where souvenir place mats with picture-perfect splashes of Martinique grace our metal dining table.

When I left Martinique after a three-week visit, I intended to go back to the island, intended to steep myself in everything I could learn about it before I returned. Strangely, the information I've been able to absorb in the sixteen months since my visit has operated to distance as much as familiarize. I'm surer now only of how little I know, how much there is to know, how impossible the goal of gaining ground, or assuming even a casual kind of authority when neither the island nor my life stand still. In the months since my first visit I've lost my father, the World Trade Center has been attacked and destroyed, I've moved from a rural area to the big city, and I've fallen deeper in love. Militant fundamentalism and right-wing electoral triumphs are reconfiguring the global political landscape, including the election of hatemonger Jean-Marie Le Pen, who won the right to oppose Jacques Chirac for the presidency of France. This is the same Le Pen who ten years before had been prevented from landing in Martinique by crowds lining the airport runway to protest his blatant racism. And how many skins has Martinique grown and shed as tides wash the island, as the sun rises over its mountains and drops flaming into the seas surrounding it?

I was offered the opportunity to go anywhere in the world and write about it. After a brief flirtation with destinations such as war zones or leper colonies or refugee camps, I decided to go someplace beautiful, where the labor of writing could be performed in pleasant surroundings. Not too far away, but someplace where I'd be challenged by feeling foreign. I'd heard Martinique was gorgeous and knew little more about the island than its similarity to Guadeloupe, a neighboring island that I had visited for a few days five or six years ago and that Patrick Chamoiseau, author of *Texaco* (one of my favorite contemporary novels), hailed from Martinique.

Why Martinique? *Why not* is always a first and sufficient reason for choosing a subject. And if the subject teaches me, if it offers enough resistance to engage and push my expressive capacities, then perhaps it's a proper subject. That readers might also be engaged, pushed, entertained and instructed by my rendering of a subject is an outcome I desire, but finally do not control.

Since French is the official language on the island, and since my companion Catherine happens to be French and willing to attempt Martinique with me, I looked forward to enjoying a kind of insider/outsider status there, my deficient French supplemented by Catherine's perfect French, our mutual ignorance of Martinique's African-derived Creole slightly less intimidating because of Creole's similarities to Afro-American vernaculars I'd grown up speaking. Thus both of us would be forced to observe, from a distance that could be informative, Martinique's mix of African and European elements—the sort of clarifying distance and difference I desired, especially since it's so difficult to achieve at home in the States, even though cultural clash, blending, and incompatibility constitute the bottom-line subjects of my writing.

Martinique is one of the Windwards, an irregular chain of islands that stretch from Puerto Rico to Venezuela at the easternmost edge of the Caribbean Sea. An overseas region of

France with French the official language, the island of Martinique as a destination for tourism is much better known and more popular in France than it is in the United States.

The Windward Islands are volcanic products of violent, fiery eruptions from steep-sided mountains rooted on the seafloor thousands of feet below the surface. Martinique's human history has been nearly as convulsive, its present culture an accretion of layers of violently displaced elements. Arawak Indians replaced Stone Age hunters and gatherers. Fierce, aggressive Carib from South America raided the Arawak, killing, kidnapping, imposing themselves and their ways till the conquered Arawak were absorbed. Beginning early in the seventeenth century, fierce, aggressive Europeans began slaughtering the Carib, securing the island for the cultivation of sugar. Africans—forcibly, brutally imported to work on sugarcane plantations—survived the holocaust of slavery. Their descendants gradually transformed Martinique's culture.

Situated between the Atlantic Ocean to the east and the Caribbean Sea to the west, Martinique's 375,000 inhabitants and 417 square miles enjoy a tropical climate and a richly variegated terrain—rugged volcanic mountains, rain forest, woods, rivers, swamps, a rocky coast, white-sand beaches. Any decent guidebook can fill you in on the island's alluring vital statistics.

The chronology on pages xv-xvi lists significant events from Martinique's past, but the narrative that follows is not intended to deliver a comprehensive account of either the island's history or its geography. As Zora Neale Hurston proclaimed in *Their Eyes Were Watching God* (a novel, by the way, that stimulated my fascination with the possibilities of vernacular speech, with Creole culture, Creole languages, Creole fiction), *You got to go there to know there.* And pay your dues.

I hope I'm providing an incentive for your journey to Martinique, and helping you imagine what might be at stake when you go. From memory I'm able to sketch a passable map of Martinique, its general shape (kidney bean or curled fetus), the major cities indicated, its topographical features roughed in. I could point out resort areas, a rust belt of fading industrial enterprises, trace my excursions to rum distilleries, slave plantations, museums and festivals staged to preserve the island's past. I can quote a few important names, dates, outline the events, periods, natural catastrophes that shaped the island's history since the French arrived in 1635.

Because I'm an American writer of African descent, I've thought about the island's function as a slave prison; brooded upon the inadequacy of African/European, black/white doubleness to account for the island's cultural complexity; theorized the island as paradise and prison, utopia and purgatory, Eden and gulag. I've been fascinated by Martinique's creative creolization of language and culture, the art of speakers and writers living and dead who have attempted to represent with words how it felt and feels to experience the island moment by moment, day by day. With my lady I've danced to the little collection of zouk CDs we purchased at an airport shop outside Fort-de-France, keeping alive in our bodies the flow, the off-beat hitch and hesitation, elegant glide and syncopated sway (slow zouk), the partying, get-down dip (hard zouk), the mellow, elegiac yearning (love zouk) of the music, music, music everywhere on the island.

I've spoken to many friendly (and a few not so friendly) Martinicans but resisted too much dependence on inside informants because my French is raggedy and unreliable, and Creole—except for nonverbal or extraverbal effects I recognize from the common African-descended core we draw from to communicate back home—stumps me. We could stop right here. Or rather, let's go ahead and keep it here. Keep it real. These facts about my intimacy with the island that I've related so far let the cat out of the bag. With a modest investment of time and effort, you could become as knowledgeable as I am about Martinique. And some of you already are Martinique. Which means you can find plenty better places to steep yourselves in Martinican facts, lore, stats. Books could be written about East Indian, Asian, or native cultures on Martinique or Muslim influences or Catholicism or island politics, subjects I've barely touched. I confess from the git-go that what I have to offer is only the record, written and rewritten, of a visit—a single visit, one visit to check out the island firsthand—and various acts of return: homage, meditation, analysis, fiction, imagining, *déjà vu,* mourning.

Revenants also signifies ghosts—the spirits who return from the dead to haunt people and places, spirits who roam past, present, and future, linking and unsettling these rigid categories of time, destabilizing our too-easy reification of impermeable boundaries between living and dead. All writers of fiction and poetry (maybe all writers period), no matter the conventions or illusions we employ, no matter how well we deploy them, are ghost writers, necromancers evoking and revitalizing the past through imagined beings, conversations, events, because our subject, what we write about, is "not present," long gone. Our labor transforms us, too, into born-again imaginary creatures, the *I, she, they, he, we, it* voices of the author's invented second-selves materializing as the reader reads and becomes, by reading and entering into a dynamic exchange, part of the imaginary also.

The places where we meet are Martiniques of one sort or another. Your Martinique is no more or less *the* Martinique than mine. The writer bestows names on persons, places, or things, then fabricates their story, and if the reader's seduced, if the transaction's effectively signed, sealed, delivered, then it partakes a bit of the sacred, the holy—that is to say, the narrative works like religion to induce belief and faith. All parties elect willingly to lose their way, are diverted by the rush of pretending to be something they are not or may be or could be, so for now, for the moment, we'll call this séance *visiting Martinique.* Let's summon *loa,* and see what we can make of the island, make of ourselves. Let's see if we can conjure up a lush island in the Caribbean, step onto the fertile soil of a country of comers-back we've visited once or never or only in a dream.

A few words about the sections following chapter 1 ("Journal"). The concept of revenants applies again, as does the idea of *creolization*—a word whose meaning will be elaborated in the text, so I'll just say that the reader should expect improvisation, spontaneity, play, breaking rules to rule here.

Writers can be the worst kind of colonizers, ruthlessly taking over and exploiting a place for their own purposes. That act of imperialism and selfish appropriation may be unavoidable, but good writing allows its subject some reciprocal prerogatives. It lets the subject, in this case Martinique, breathe, plant its flag, articulate its claim, inhabit the writer's territory.

While experiencing Martinique's novelty, uniqueness, and resistance, I've tried to open myself to this difference. The parts of this book, with their various modes of narrative representation, are attempts to allow myself to be invaded, to live in other skins, to assume risks. Encourage the island to problematize, call into question who I am and who I'm not.

> The distinctive historical experiences of [the African] diaspora's populations have created a unique body of reflections on modernity and its discontents which is an enduring presence in the cultural and political struggles of their descendants today.
>
> —PAUL GILROY, *The Black Atlantic*

I am not, never was, a slave, and slavery has been legally abolished on the island since 1848, yet slavery's shadow, as metaphor, as history and prophecy, as living heritage on Martinique influenced my understanding of the island, of myself—who I am, who I might become.

Nor have I ever owned slaves or managed slaves—"managed" a polite word for the power to compel other human beings, under the threat of pain or death, to execute my will—but that power, particularly its abuses, intrigues me. Whether in the context of a plantation or prison or concentration camp, how does the exercise of absolute authority change us—the powerful and the powerless. Through Père Labat (1663-1738), a Dominican priest who sailed to Martinique in 1693 and lived there for a dozen years, author of a chronicle of his island sojourn that is still in print, widely read and highly praised today, I've attempted to investigate the seduction of unfettered license, the extremes of violence and compulsion we perpetrate on one another.

Père Labat gained great renown as the manager of an enormously profitable, church-owned, slaveholding sugarcane plantation and rum distillery, similar to the Habitation Latouche visited in chapter 4 of this book. His mind was a bizarre mix of the scientific rationalism of his era and medieval superstition. Labat believed Africans to be the devil's natural children, capable of sorcery. He vouches for the veracity of (and delights in recounting) extraordinary demonstrations of Africans' occult powers: a boy who conjures rain by chanting, then poking sticks in oranges he's arranged in a mystical pattern on the ground; a woman whose ability to dry up the hearts of her enemies is proved by autopsies that reveal the victims' desiccated organs.

Ironically, in a delicious creolized twist, Père Labat—an actual historical figure from Martinique's past—became embedded in the island's folk history as a bogeyman and hobgoblin. Because of his reputation for cruelty and evil caprice, Père Labat's name was invoked by parents to scare misbehaving children. *"Mi! Moin ké fai Pé Labatt vini pouend ou—oui!* (I'll make Père Labat come and take you away!)" After discovering the many ways Labat left his imprint—from establishment hero in the economic development of the island to spectral villain in the counterculture of Creole memory—I couldn't resist a brief foray (chapter 2) into the priest's mind.

The Katrine and John of the Journal (chapter 1) experience a love on Martinique that survives the island generally intact and may (I hope) continue to flourish. Obviously not all island romances fare as well when forced to negotiate a society bearing slavery's scars—continuing racial prejudice, segregation, and oppression—to say nothing of dealing with the antagonistic oppositions of Europe and Africa, white and black, male and female, rich and poor, tourist and dispossessed, different languages. And of course there's maybe the worst pitfall of them all to overcome, the individual differences forming and informing each of us.

I couldn't help imagining a virtual couple I baptized Chantal and Paul (very similar in ways to Katrine and John) whose love floundered in encountering the real odds against it abounding on any Martinique. I can't say exactly why I needed Paul and Chantal—you may have your guesses—but I know my invention arose partly as a negative talisman to ward off my ancient fear of losing what's most precious and partly from the visceral, visual presence of loss and waste, the haunted, deadly past alive in Martinique's music, dance, arts, speech, faces—sweet but always also wistful, fragile, temporary, elusive, *islanded.*

In chapter 3, against the background of the words of Frantz Fanon (1925-1961)—a Martinique-born writer, philosopher, psychiatrist, and a hero in Algeria's war for independence from France, prescient critic of colonialism, violence, and love—

I composed the love story of Chantal and Paul, inventing what happened to them, but they also infiltrated, instructed, helped compose—as *what could have been* always does—the story that was real for Katrine and John.

Chapter 4, titled The Island, is a return—a single sentence taking the narrative back to its beginnings in the Journal and bringing this whole business of visiting, touring, past and present forward to the moment you read it.

> Martinique is the island that carries on the most beautiful commerce as judged by the large number of vessels that always abound here and by the fertility of its land, which produces beautiful sugar, cotton, coffee, etc. This island furnishes all the other windward isles ... and gives them an outlet for all that they produce ... St.-Pierre is a place so famous for its commerce that each year more than 300 ships arrive in this harbor loaded with merchandise that sells so well that they return to France loaded with sugar and cotton.
>
> —ROBERT DURANT,
> quoted in *The Diligent* by Robert Harms

Durant—a Frenchman serving as an officer on a slaving ship that sailed from Vannes in France to Africa, then to Martinique and back to France—wrote the words above in his journal as he awaited his voyage home in 1731. Like Père Du Tertre a century before, he paints an idyllic picture of Martinique—idyllic if you ignore, as they do, the central place of human cargoes in "the most beautiful commerce." Such elisions, contradictions, and ironies point to the difficulties of portraying a place, any place, all places that are never more or less than the sum total of the witness borne by those who lived there. Witness in the form of tangible records we can consult, or silent witness we can only imagine.

CHAPTER ONE

Journal

25 December 2000

This trip to an island begins—as if it's a story or a dream—on Christmas Day, a day, a time of year overbearingly fraught with symbolism, with memories and images no matter how familiar, obvious, and drained of meaning, that still wash over us, immerse us, drown us in sentimentality and nostalgia and regret. So in spite of our disbelief, the formulaic wishes for health or prosperity or joy tendered back and forth sound good, seem appropriate if momentary lapses into other times—mythic times, better times past or future, when hope, though thin, might stretch a little further, might redeem (or cushion at least) the daily unavoidable blows of a perilous world. Whatever else happens during this year-end wintry time of ritual and actual dying, the season always is (and as long as human beings exist will be) a time of birth for someone somewhere, and who knows what those new eyes will see or disclose, so *Joyeux Noël, Feliz Navidad,* Merry Christmas.

Anyone in whatever culture or language starting a story in a season like Christmas or Easter that commemorates the year's perpetual rhythm would be aware of all of the above or know more or believe differently but could not ignore the baggage—the resonance begged, borrowed, or stolen—if she or he begins in a season when Earth dies a little, on the eve of what the West celebrates as the birth of a militant savior-prince so high, mighty, and holy that His name would conquer time, would alter time, and that time ever after would be adorned with His name—B.C. before Him, A.D. after—the Christian New Year celebrated the week after His birth, time divided in two by His coming, two different kinds of time, different dispensations, as distinct, some claim, as the multiple creations of man must have been—white, black, brown, red, yellow—to account for the distinguishing characteristics of each so-called "race," the divinely ordained hierarchy from inferior to superior.

First, darkness covers the Earth, then Christ appears and light bursts upon the Old World. Upon the people suffering in ignorance, wallowing in animal pleasures and pagan pride. Christ's coming splits time wide open and drags the people forth, screaming, struggling, from the black womb of night, a flock unworthy of His touch, His loving care, but needing the light, needing His promise of redemption, of peace, needing pain and remorse and duty and fear, the intractable letters of His law, *Give me your tired, poor, and hungry, A mind is a terrible thing to waste, God Save the King, Give it up this morning, sisters and brothers.* This Christ robed in a milk-white mantle in whose name humankind has committed every conceivable cruelty upon itself, a creed no better or worse than others, I suppose, that grant believers permission to treat nonbelievers worse than dogs, creeds whose tangled heaps of prohibitions, incitements, and license pile up mountain high and we spend far too much of our precious time on Earth groveling up, groveling under them. I'm tired of it this morning, the bullshit, the drama, and resolve to shed my own chilly, bone-white garment, awakening in the tropics, the "sad tropics," anthropologist Claude Lévi-Strauss called this sun and sea and verdant jungle and scouring, caressing, soporific deadly wind.

I waken smelling of sex, one eye half-closed by its coat of dried gravy, the *métissage* of our sticky juices and moist-lipped cavities, Creole wine pressed from the grapes of our dancing, grappling bodies. I'm alone now, in a chair, outdoors on a balcony, sweating again already at this early hour. Drops of sweat splat on this page. Imagine the sound the word "splat" attempts to render, the luminous emissaries the sounds of words would be if they could.

Splat.

Is that the sound of a drop of sweat absorbed by the cottony quiet page, the page also holding within itself the ghost screams of trees toppled by power saws, trees squashed and steamrollered thin as skin, vast Amazonian forests mourned now by this mute page, a stillness that smothers all the woodland glade noises animating the Martinique terrace where I sit this Christmas morning in the sad tropics. Present sounds silenced as if the breeze has picked the air clean, swept away every bird twitter and insect buzz from the dense green pulse just palpable of luxuriant tropical vegetation always growing, spreading, encroaching closer and closer even as you scan what seems to be its swaying, deep-rooted immobility, its baroque profusion framing the margins of your gaze, a forest one thousand miles distant leveled by bulldozers, pulped, compressed, squeezed into yellow sheets inked with blue lines and the many identical sheets stacked and glued, one after another bound into this pad I'm using that costs next to nothing in the supermarket so almost anyone can purchase one, own one and scribble to his or her heart's content or use sheets of paper to wipe your ass, your snot, sop up your tears or blood with gauzy tissues so handy and disposable you can afford to spoil pages with your aborted words, your drops of sweat, you can keep turning, it never ends, to the next and next clean sheet that docilely bears somehow, somewhere deep inside itself the anguish of a rain forest and all the creatures inhabiting it howling, the deer, salamanders, hibiscus, spiders, the naked, ox-eyed Indians.

"Air Caraibes" is inscribed on the bulkhead partitioning the 757's ergonomically sculpted interior in which we're packed, middle passage spoon fashion, on the last short hop from one island to another. A lamentable, pitiable but also funny sort of hubris displayed by the act of keeping alive the tribal name of a people you slaughtered, my airline hosts, the Carib from whom you stole this land, massacring, scattering thousands of the native people, until a hundred years ago the volcano Soufrière, as Carib prophecies had foretold, wiped out in a pyroclastic surge the final band of Carib hiding in the rugged mountains of the island of St. Vincent. A reckless, bottomless arrogance manifests itself, my hosts, in your preservation of the evidence of your guilt—like a mad serial killer who curates a grisly archive of his conquests, locks of hair, bits of dried flesh, a tooth, bloody panties, an ear, a thigh bone, the impeccable unspeakable unimpeachable proof against himself he can't help storing in the basement of his suburban, split-level bungalow, the museum to which he's drawn irresistibly to prowl, sniff and finger the booty he knows someday, in some court will convict him, seal his doom.

"Caribbean." From the ashes of one name, one old *béké* joke a new people arose, another irony birthed. Africans captured, coffled, purchased, packed into the holds of cargo ships, imported to the New World in droves. African names expunged. Slaves branded like cattle, tagged with pet names. Any old rag-tag fragment and ruin and rune and scab of name. Darky in the Mirror names: Angélique, Thérèse, Dominique, François, Armand, Cécile. Ironic, show-off-the-master's-learning (or the slave's yearning) names: Caesar, Archimedes, Plato, Philomène, Sybèle. Blackening names: Cudjoe, Rastas. Names ripe for latter-day Creole bricolage, hybridity, humor, irony to recontextualize, rephrase, relexify, restore to the bearers of hurting names their self-worth, dignity, power, humanity. A rummage sale, charnel house, carnival of appellations for property like people, people like property. With a stroke of his gavel the auctioneer, the bestower of value and names, severs the Old World from the New. Anything goes. Everything goes. Going. Going. Gone. Sold to the gentleman, sold to the lady with the red dress on. Shake it, don't break it, sweet thang.

Welcome to the tropics. The New South. Air Caraibes. Fun

in the sun for everyone. A new world order cleansed of doubt, shadow, guilt, history. A new multiculture that's monolingual, monochrome, monological. A society in which variety defers to dominance and dominance neuters variety. You're free to choose your tribal name, tribal label: West Indian, Martinican, Black, *béké,* Nigger, French. We're all Caribbean here.

So why not me, here on tour, eligible as anyone else to enjoy the island. Didn't my ancestors sacrifice buckets of blood as a down payment so I too could travel to this site of Europe's ruthless embracing and erasure of Africanness. This threshing ground and screaming, winnowing, seasoning place. Cash register. Cash cow for France, England, and their enemies when one or another of their less powerful, smaller neighbors snatched for a day or year one of these sugary territories. Haiti. Guadeloupe. Martinique. These emerald Antilles set in a blazing sea. What is Africa to me.

I'm free at last to enjoy the spoils. Cook in the tropical heat day after day, get blacker till I split one afternoon, like a raisin in the sun. Prodigal son returned. High John the Conqueroo with his lady, be she black or white or some green-eyed, beige in-betweener—no one seems to give a flying fuck as long as my credit card computes, the numbers rising into the azure void of the heavens almost as fast as the speed of light, networking, interfacing, alchemizing from the nothingness of that empty blue empyrean miracles of instant gratification, wine, water, music, clothes, meals, shelter, sex on demand if the numbers are willing, if they climb fast and far, almost as fast as the dreams of old Africans who, clambering out of the boiling surf, continuing their ancient journey, disembarking daily on these shores, chained, greased, half-starved, puking, chanting, willing themselves instantly elsewhere, Africans shape-shifting, escaping the whips, the searing blue of their captors' eyes. Dark, invisible ghosts moaning in the machinery of this island, this garden, these resorts drawing us here from hither and yon, scattering us, splattering us like the salty drops of sweat that soundlessly expire on the page. *Splat.* And in that barely perceptible sound, if we could render it, lies the ... But we've tried, we've been there before and it takes us nowhere except to the scouring, erasing wind, loud surf battering against ashy old black stick legs churning one last league through unnavigable waves to shore. Here. Where we are. Lamenting, stunned by how easy, after all, it's been. To fly cross an ocean and arrive here. To return. To be lost, lost, lost in the ether, the virtual, imagined congress of east and west, north and south, the adulterous intercourse, the one-way dialogue of black and white, of separation and synthesis, of speed and silence and simpering, simmering Creole protest. The irresistible order of things. The topsy-turvy of dialectic forbidden. First always first and last always last. The imperial imposition of a single, hypnotic monotone to trump all other voices, the breathless, unending narrative of desire trivialized and reduced to buying what's offered for sale on the island.

We drop out of the sky. We are washed up out of the sea. Our black mammies squat and piss us onto the damp sand. We are vulnerable, wet and glistening as the eggs of sea turtles. Thus we land here, my brethren, my sisters, born again on blistering tarmac. A sedate calypso piped from unseen speakers rhythms our progress, our promenade under long canopies of plastic awnings, striped sky-blue and white, shunting us into the duty-free holding area. Where it all begins. Began. Ends. Does it matter.

26 DECEMBER 2000

Katrine commenced to leak red slowly this morning, her bloody greeting to the island, her farewell to the child we would never conceive, letting go, loosing from her womb the phantom child's liquid flesh and bones, a melancholy soup mixing, scenting the other fluids our bodies had seeped the night before. A quiet, stark, bitter musk where her legs come together and part. When I washed her there with a warm, damp cloth, I didn't want the scent to disappear. Wanted it to cling subtly to my fingertips. I'm far too old to consider siring more children and Katrine's lush body, though tight and young as a girl's, had reached the cusp where even if she could bear more children, why subject herself to the stress and trauma, why push a point, why prove again the certain knowledge her body had revealed eleven years before, carrying Romeo, her golden son, pushing the gift of him perfectly formed, perfectly nourished and hungry into the world.

We hadn't been trying for a child, but one night in November the Earth had moved for both of us and in the tumult of stillness immediately afterward, for some reason, we'd both thought the same thought. Damn, it was some good shit, wasn't it, and damn, what if we'd just made a baby. In our playfulness, the almost bragging mood of shared joy and absolute escape from the ordinary we'd managed to pull off thrashing about in each other, we had invented Martinique's roller-coaster mountain roads before we'd seen them, a landscape we rode as we spun it from damp, silvery filaments shot through secret piercings in our flesh.

In the happy confusion of being disarranged and disoriented and suddenly very far away, then miraculously returning, the Earth solid under us again, both of us intact on a slightly mildewed mattress identifying the particular room, the crummy hotel, the city where we found ourselves that November night, our minds still in synch, mapping out more familiar turf, remembering our names, the planet's name, the galaxy, the name of the month, date, and time, Katrine had voiced the thought that had popped into both our minds, yes, a baby could have happened. Not very likely, but yes, she'd been smack-dab in the middle of her cycle, the briar patch of most fertile days, and then last night, our first on the island, experiencing again those sensations we'd felt in November, the shock of falling off the edge of the Earth, that explosion and bump and hollering sigh of relief, like a hanged man jiggling, gasping, his own muscles squeezing him to death until every taut cord releases and he's free, free at last, but we'd survived the rope again last night, ten days past the time her very regular period due and still no signs, not a trickle afterward so both of us wondering without saying a word what it might mean if in fact she was carrying my seed, the prospect real enough now to be less abstract than *seed,* to be an imminent daughter or son we'd have to choose a name for, love, diaper, feed, send to college, a new being (possibly the color of the solar system, since astronomers recently announced our chunk of universe would appear beige when seen from a great distance) who could change the world, launch the world into another dimension as swiftly, utterly, sweetly, beyond belief and forgiveness as we'd launched ourselves elsewhere, fucking and *maybe maybe* as highly unlikely, cruelly unlikely as such a possibility might be, perhaps in our fumbling, in our pleasure, we'd begotten a child.

27 December 2000

Not to be, of course. Not really. Absolutely not here, as you concede, more sober today, more somber after Katrine's small lapse into tears, the small shudders for a minute or two yesterday when she leaned into your shoulder and wrapped your arms around herself, no new life starting on this island. You're learning its long history of refusal. No union, no unity, no amalgamation. The island's persistent either/or, black or white, work or die, *forsake all hope* message to slaves. Its postslavery denial of dreams. Promises broken. Promise crushed in African-descended natives. Its encouragement and scorn of daydreams.

I'm sorry, Katrine. I didn't know how much it mattered.

Please, she said. Don't speak, she said. I just want to sit quiet a minute.

This beguiling island with a chip on its shoulder. Its heavy-handed cruelty and barbarity. A lost child. Why would it miss one more lost child. One who never was. I thought

Katrine and I had been playing a game the last week or so. Making up a virtual child. Riffing on a very minuscule possibility. Teasing each other about the implausible lives we'd lead after it arrived. The whole business funny because unthreatening. A conceit, a little joke spicing our intimate exchanges.

The island called Katrine. The island called John. The island called John. The island called Katrine. Called John. Called Katrine. John/Katrine. Katrine/John. Calling. Being called. Separate islands. Floating. Merging.

First is birth, last is death. And what shall we call this in-between island. This Martinique. Where we drift—neither and both. Where we discover we have only each other after dreaming the almost comic accident or nearly tragic happenstance of a child we could have conceived. A couple weeks of fanciful speculating. Is Katrine's belly slightly swollen. Pouting like lips pout after kissing and sucking for hours. A cute little pot-au-feu simmering in her flat stomach. She rubs it, grins, cradles air in two hands, and rocks the baby. Mama's baby. Daddy's maybe, I tease her. How do I know what you've got in there belongs to me, girl. Hope you have the cell-phone number of the Kilroy Negro been sneaking in my back door, girl. Biff-bam, thank you mamming you. Hope he owns a cell phone and ain't in no cell owns him. One of those headed-for-the-hills maroon Negroes absconding with the goodies, runaway, runaway, leaving behind a trail of chicken feathers from the squawky hen he's got squeezed under one arm, trail of hard, black little turds from the greasy piglet tucked under the other, half the smokehouse in a sack he's appropriating as partial down payment on back wages owed him, runagate, runagate, hopped up from my lady's bed, gone out the back window wearing nothing but a long, funky-tailed shirt, his black hide. Didn't look back once at the big house he'd burn to the ground in a minute if he had a match, if he had a minute to spare from the particulars of escaping, from cradling and coo-cooing and throttling noisy *livestock* he's ripping off. He'd torch the white-pillared, sulfur-smelling *grande maison* if he was sure he wasn't leaving behind a golden child in miss white lady's belly or a brown gal's bed, Daddy's baby, maybe, ashes, ashes, when the *béké's* crib goes tumbling down in flames.

Months later Katrine will tell me she's sure she was pregnant, excess blood a miscarriage, but this azure morning after we sleep in late then spend most of the afternoon sitting up in bed, listening to the sea, to storms faked by palm fronds rustling, the main topic of conversation our ... what ... our relationship, affair, good luck, whatever, and neither of us mention the child who never happened. Something too serious about the make-believe surrounding that nonevent. The game has played itself out and neither of us wants to admit how real then quickly unreal things can be. Everything changing in the twinkling of an eye. The lost child a missing chapter in the narrative we string together this afternoon. So much occurring so suddenly between us we need a story, don't we, to prop up what feels fragile, vulnerable. Finding ourselves here on this island happy beyond words but also worrying that what we've found might suddenly disappear. We're haunted by imagined grief, anticipated wounds we have no words for either, except "lost child," words we can't say. You bring nothing to the island. Take nothing away.

In my recollection, for what it's worth, when we encountered each other the first time, no lightning crackled, no thunder rumbled, no second-sighted certainty, no doomed, obsessive fatal attraction. The conference in Cancun ended. We flew home to separate cities, countries, destinies. Months passed. We shuttled through other lovers' arms before we met again. A hectic period in my life, the sad aftermath of a thirty-year marriage, remorse, guilt, hassling with lawyers and endless depressing details, little sleep, bumbling around in a kind of fog seeping from scattered pieces of lives no longer fitting together, a sense that I had failed one good woman and thereby probably disqualified myself for any other, yet still a strong desire to see Katrine again. The first evening of a five-day conference in Mexico, I'd recited something to her on the way to dinner, my words smeared by the wind, her hair blowing in her face, natives of different languages, so not much of what I was saying got through, but Katrine's a generous spirit and recalls a sort of poetry, something flowing, rhythmic anyway, fitting the moment, helped by the fact that we were strolling along a flowered path beside the sea, and to tell the truth, I don't remember exactly what words I paraphrased or quoted or improvised on the spot, just that I wanted to impress, to let the lady know she was special in my eyes, that someone who spoke and smiled and walked like her, one strong, shapely leg revealed to the thigh with each stride splitting her long black dress, fit exactly my idea of the person with whom I'd want to share lots of moments like the one we'd stumbled upon, strangers, yes, for now, but maybe not complete strangers since people strongly attracted never are really strangers.

Looking back you could say we drifted together, clicked, then drifted apart, but I also believe there was an imperceptible current, irresistible perhaps, in what seemed to be a placid, nodding sea, a current or purposeful breeze directing us toward each other, toward another opportunity to greet and learn and wonder and be changed.

She lets me rattle on, then, now, telling the story as if I'm speaking for her, too. Then I notice she's stopped paying attention—her eyes staring out the window at palm fronds scratching each others' backs.

We say *coup de foudre.* For me, for most people I know, love always starts with a coup de foudre.

Love at first sight. First glance.

No. Nothing so stupid. A coup is very strong, very deep. You know when it hits you. You know you must have the other person. You ache for them. Love may not happen after a coup. It's not about after. It's how you must feel to begin.

Her blue eyes are flashing a green challenge at me. Angry then sad. Sad, angry at the thought I might not have experienced what she experienced. And I'm instantly alarmed and hurt by the possibility she might believe I love her less than she loves me just because I couldn't claim I'd heard the MGM orchestra explode the first time we laid eyes on each other. I admitted again the lacerating downslide and seemingly terminal despondency surrounding that time in Mexico had prevented me from paying proper attention to what had transpired between us. Assured her I'm struck by precisely that species of thunder and lightning, stunned to my toes, shaken as if all the trumpets of Zion blowing down Jericho's walls, yes, just like in

Hollywood movies, uh huh, a sho-nuff coup de foudre, if not exactly once at the beginning, many, many times since, daily maybe, my eyes, my heart overwhelmed, moved at the center of my being again and again, excitement and desire thrilling me, filling me at any given moment, like now, this very instant, you standing naked in the bathroom door accusing me, doubting me, those blue-green eyes on my case, abusing me about some allegedly missing coup de foudre.

I understand finally that whatever I said would only make things worse so I try to switch the subject, switching without really losing the subject, the thread, the lifeline I need to pull myself back into her good graces. Not a trick, really. Because I'm telling the truth.

I guess you could say old Christopher Columbus got hit by a coup. I guess he sure enough believed himself destiny's child when the thunder and lightning of sailing west to go east hit him. Maybe that's why he was so cocksure, so crazy.

Columbus who on one of his voyages west to discover east heard rumors of this very island, *Matinino* he called it in his journal. An "Indian told me of the island ... farther to the east of Caribe, and said that it is inhabited only by women, and on it is a great deal of *tuob,* which is gold or copper." Six days later he notes his continuing interest: "On this course I would find the island of Matinino, which is inhabited only by women. I would like to carry five or six of them to the sovereigns." But when he reached the island during a subsequent voyage (June 15, 1502) he didn't pay too much attention to Martinique, one more beautiful green island in a sea full of beautiful islands. Stupid, stupid-ass Columbus just sent a boat and some sailors to fetch fresh water, gather fruit, reminding his men to be alert for inhospitable, man-eating Indians. Columbus, struck by his coup de foudre, never ceased perceiving himself as royalty on a divine mission, even when his destiny becalmed for years by sargassos of bad weather, bad karma, bad judgment, he never doubted fate also was relentlessly driving a plot line that would crown him with fame and riches beyond imagination. Columbus who could endure disappointment after disappointment, island after island inhabited only by naked Indios, liars with hairdos like the priests, Indios who died too easily under questioning, taking their secrets with them, if secrets they contained, if secrets or any sense whatever resided in the beast babble of savage tongues—languages that the lying, spying linguists he's forced to include on his trips pretended to understand. The rumored secrets—cities of gold, fountains whose waters confer youth, islands of women—were make-believe, he'd come to believe, flimsy as those airy fictions of the simpering padres who asserted their authority over these poor creatures by claiming the Indians possessed souls. Columbus enduring decades of exile from court, mischief, backbiting and slanders at home, the arduous bloodletting and torture required to extract truth from the natives and finding no gold, no cloud-capped towers, no eternal youth, no men whose heads grow beneath their shoulders, only profitless green islands inhabited by slavish, thick-skulled brown monkeys, but the Great Navigator, Admiral of the Seven Seas, enthralled by the soap-opera fate he imagined for himself, let nothing deter him, not day after seafaring day of misery, not mutiny in his dwindling crew and his own mortified flesh. He endured it all to tune in each day, same time, same station because this could be the day the dog-eared lottery ticket in his pocket would deliver the prize.

The Governor-General, Commandante, Generalissimo, El Presidente pressed on, never faltering, his resolve pure, relentless, the Great Emancipator who freed the Old World from ignorance of the New, secure in the knowledge of his progress toward vindication and happy-ever-after, and the two of us, Katrine, will we prove as tough as old, single-minded, vile-smelling, crusty, naughty, greedy, evil-tempered Columbus, pushing on, or love drawing us on, neither of us privy to any grand design. No vision of a promised land. With uncountable perils and obstacles ahead, will we be as lucky/unlucky as blind Columbus and blunder onto the shores of a New World.

The pregnant business unfunny, even soberingly serious for a while, but the farfetched chance Katrine might be carrying a child also opens the door for a bizarre turn, and laughing, finding some foolishness even in the most gruesome circumstance, the rug pulled out unexpectedly from a poor soul's feet (our feet, too) no matter the victim's misery, laughing in spite of the fact disaster rules, a survival technique Katrine and I shared. We both cultivated an appreciation of the absurd, relished the perverse power to smile about what's beyond our control, our imagining, whether ridiculous or awful. A sort of hoodoo against the worst, affirming helpless surprise or shock with laughter. Then again, sometimes, you can't stop the joke from turning back on itself, back on you, laughter and foolishness rushing away like your breath if someone sneaks up and whoops you across the belly with a baseball bat. African messenger gods occasionally mix up their instructions, lift us to the stars before they realize their mistake and empty us like a bucket of night-soil into the sea.

Maybe, maybe, baby, but not really. Not here where centuries of spilled blood drips heavily into the soil *splat splat* and the cheap thrill of supposing otherwise is just that—a thrill—cheap. To think that this once, this seed, this child could be conceived against the odds and drop from the sky into our wide-open arms, our wide-open hearts, our wide eyes glued to the streak of its falling arc, our feet planted firmly to absorb the blow of its landing.

I envision the dark, towering superstructure of an Egyptian galley, Ra's great ship anchored at night, the moon backlighting its curved prow, a small boat gliding from under the skirt of the ship's shadow, the small raft's steady progress in spite of being tossed by wind and waves, as if propelled by a bank of oars. Is there a magic current propelling it, guiding it, calming the fears of its single occupant curled in a basket set on a wide board running the length of the boat's hull, like a spine where its ribs attach. The fierceness of the wind also holds the soothing echo of a mother singing, the promise of her breast and the chance this passage across dangerous waters may end somewhere, somehow, peacefully perhaps in that very mother's arms, the lost child recovering a name she whispers, inheriting the country she rules, a land a thousand times wealthier than the fabled Indies, her teeming land, rich as black loam of her womb, sweet as her white milk's stickiness on the child's tongue.

Katrine dreamed last night a woman impregnated her. An acquaintance from years back whose name she can't recall. Dreamed I'd been unfaithful to her in Atlanta, Georgia.

Katrine. Katrine. I'm doggy-pleading in the dream. Don't be upset, baby. Don't leave me. Didn't mean nothing. Nothing, baby. Just a fling. I don't even remember her name.

One odd dream after another steals her sleep. Gobbles her peace. Exhaustion feeding on itself like a starving body cannibalizes its own flesh and blood. My nightmare like a rerun of a familiar documentary I've never seen. Manstealers armed with guns, sabers, whips drive a coffle of naked, chained Africans through dense jungle. The column has reached the point when drivers and driven are exhausted, no longer believe they'll reach the sea, the forced march self-destructing, eating itself like the weariness consuming Katrine's sleep. We trudge from dawn to dusk, stop only to unmanacle the dead from the living and the living gain a brief respite to let the dead tumble into thick elephant grass at the edges of the trail, the way the dead tossed overboard from slaving ships segue silently into the sea, barely a ripple, this tithing, this ironic salvation, this sharing the spoils, the manstealers' offerings to shark gods, jackal gods, ant gods, fly gods whose boundless appetite sneers at a measly one in ten, demands more, demands all.

In a strange language I cannot speak yet understand, the one chained to me asks, are we making progress, getting closer. Closer to what, my eyes reply. The nasty, skimpy port towns with their false glitter, stone-walled forts, the cattle pens where they'll lodge us, waiting for a bright sail to pop over the horizon and carry us away.

So much already lost, perhaps all lost, we suffer that truth as we march on and marching on is another truth, another god to serve or deny. Gods never assuaged, never swayed by our weeping, our moaning. We fear the gods because they can read our minds, our hearts. We hope as we struggle another step and another, they will see our sorrow isn't false. We're not trying to trick them. A portion of each of us dies when the other dies, even if the fallen one is only imagined, fancied, because such an imagined one is truth also, ourselves conceiving ourselves as other. Like the wish to be better we stake in love. The dream of combining with another soul and from our incompleteness, from our failures, mistakes, disappointments, from the two of us perhaps create another, a better person, or create different selves—Katrine and John, John and Katrine. Our old names and colors fading, blending, releasing someone new. After drifting together, drifting apart, surging together once more, will we invent another chance on this island.

After a rocky night, after a storm of chatter, of longing and need and regret and fear too deep to speak of, the two of us together on a bed in a rented room, in a tropical resort in a fractured universe, imagining the sound of a small boat inching through the night sea toward paradise.

28 December 2000

Of course the bouncing, skimpy, drunken little boat doesn't make it. I listened all night for Katrine's blood to stop flowing. Another nonevent. Like dreaming a dream in a dream in a dream. That's all the child was, after all. Get over it. Return to what's real. Somebody popped the paper bag we'd tenderly inflated. Pop. Pow. Boom. Ghost frigates bombarding an insomniac fortress, Martinique's old capital, Port Royal. Iron balls thudding noisily, harmlessly against the stones. No penetration, not even dents. Like flies colliding with a screen, bump bump bump in the night. The stony ramparts sleep soundly through the storm while civilians and soldiers roam the besieged city's narrow streets all night. Wandering along rows of closed shops, bumping into each other in the darkness, afraid to light candles, lanterns, street lamps, afraid any sign of life visible from the harbor will guide the enemy's cannon. At dawn Port Royal's weary colons collapse, sprawl in heaps at the shadowed corners of buildings, under awnings, pilfering any shade they can scrounge to protect themselves from the scorching tropical sun. Eternal siesta. Total exhaustion and fear. Fear of capture, of contamination, of breaches in the fortress's stone walls, the prison within the prison of their waking nightmare: the world topsy-turvy, black over white, themselves slaves, chained, incarcerated, worked to death in blazing fields of cane, prisoners of marauding pirates who blast away all night at the barricaded town, swarthy barbarians speaking incomprehensible baa-baa-baa languages, cruel strangers who herd them into galleys, transport them *outre-mer* to a faraway wilderness. Loose them naked into the forest's boundlessness, into time with no beginning or end. No clothes, no clocks, no names, no gods, just tasks and duties rhythmed by whips brandished in dark fists.

Trekking in late afternoon up a steep hill on our way to the village of Ste.-Anne, Katrine informs me that in Paris there's a huge mental hospital called Ste.-Anne's, and that saying someone's "headed to Ste.-Anne's" is slang for signifying he or she is nuts. About three-quarters of the way to Ste.-Anne, just about at the end of the long haul up, we're rewarded with a spectacular view (officially certified as a *belle vue*—Bellevue, by the way, a large mental hospital in New York City—on a plaque fastened to an iron railing) of the coastline, the *grande anse* or basket handle in whose deep curve Ste.-Anne rests, the town a small clutter of streets and roofs interrupting a golden edging of beach and behind the sand a dense pelt of forest, then rolling hills, cultivated into rectangles of various shades of green and beyond that steeper hills sink into the glimmering bay and farther, softened by the blue haze of distance, silhouetted against the horizon, are hulking mounds like the bodies of giants rising from or plunging into the sea, far away where the water loses its blinding sparkle and turns to mist shrouding these creatures sounding its depths.

Ahead, on the crest of this hill leading to Ste.-Anne, I notice people spilling from one side to the other of the street we're ascending. Cars helter-skelter on road and sidewalk cram every inch of available parking space between us and the crest. The crowd—brown people wearing clothes—means they're locals, not tourists. Closer, I can see the people blocking the road are dressed in combinations of black and white. Black suit, white shirt, black tie. Ankle-length black skirt, starched white blouse. Various combinations of vests, jackets, slacks, dresses, shirts riffing on the theme of black and white and I presume checkerboard harmonies must be traditional for mourning because on the right side of the sidewalk, the seaside dropping off steeply to the bay, just beyond a shoulder-high white wall topped by a metal rail, a cemetery comes into view. Now I see the crowd's milling beside a gate opening into the white wall and inside the wall a profusion of cross-crowned, above-ground tombs, gleaming white vaults packed as tightly inside the cemetery as the cars along the curb, as slaves in the middle passage. The tombs remind me of fancy bathrooms and kitchens in home-decorating magazines. Spotless porcelain, marble, and tile, black grout to emphasize the symmetry, the orderliness and purity of white squares. But these are not sinks and toilets and shower stalls, are they. On a flat shelf cut into the sloping hillside, surrounded by a wall white as the sepulchers it encloses, a mini-city of the dead, incorruptible boxes housing the corrupting remains of citizens who hiked up the street before us, smiled at the *belle vue,* skirted the bright cemetery we pass on the way to Ste.-Anne.

On just about every available surface—the stone laps, shoulders, and bosoms, the stair-stepped headboards of oblong boxes where crosses are mounted—offerings of flowers have been tossed, stacked, laid with care, single flowers, bunches of flowers, unruly heaps, elaborate memorial set pieces professionally arranged and placed, flowers beribboned, flowers scattered, crushed, a record perhaps of a recent holiday or feast, the tropical gaudiness and frivolity of dying blossoms every color of the rainbow jostling with the strict, cold geometry of white-tiled tombs for dominance of the site. Some vaults near enough to reach out and touch as we continue up the hill.

The burying ground's baroque architecture clamors for attention. Miniature houses with porticoes, porches, carved figures, stairs flanked by vases and urns, the grandiose dimensions of some monuments, the irregular skyline of crosses, peaked roofs, steeples, obelisks, all competing to be nearer, nearer to God than their neighbors. Despite all that visual noise and the flamboyantly dying flowers, the silence on the other side of the wall is deep as the bottom of a bottomless well. The houses of the dead so near and far. Where is *"ce pays des sans-chapeaux."* Is it just over there beyond your shoulder, equal but separate. Why so quiet? Why do I feel I could blink and all the stone monuments would disappear, the speeches, aspirations, and vanity embodied in them a chimera, the heaviness of lifetimes of memory weightless as a passing thought, like my thought that the cemetery, the dead it silences and hides could blink and I'd be invisible wandering in a strange land where hats aren't needed anymore.

I have the urge to hang around here where the cemetery gate opens and the mourners congregate. I want to observe, ask questions, take notes, eavesdrop on conversations. I'm sure I'll learn something important in spite of my language handicap. Learn Martinican techniques for formalizing and taming grief. Learn who's dead. Learn who these people are for whom the dead one matters. I would stop, mix in with the mourners except I don't want to appear like a tourist. Obnoxious, intrusive, an unconnected outsider, temporary, phony, demanding, superior, irrelevant like a tourist.

But isn't that exactly what we are, Katrine asks later. Tourists. And what's wrong with being a tourist, anyway. Can't people be tourists without being assholes.

Next morning I push Katrine's point further. Maybe being a tourist provides a useful metaphor for anybody's sojourn here on Earth. Isn't everybody's presence here, there, anywhere, a sort of accident that unhappens when they die. Aren't we all strays (from where), strangers touring strange lands. The ritual we'd bumped into as we mounted the hill to Ste.-Anne not only about properly disposing of the mortal remains of the freshly dead, but an acknowledgment that every tour ends by introducing a familiar stranger, one who, as we all now understand, never intended to stay. The tour ends unfinished, ends elsewhere, nowhere, ends no closer to home. Like uncountable Africans kidnapped here to work and die, this newly dead one has vanished, passed on to whatever, if anything, comes next. Touring heaven. Touring the interminable blackness inside these whitened boxes. Touring their own sea-changed flesh, bone, oceans of fluids, miles of singing cords, the millions of gates, windows, doors through which, quick as light, the body's current speeds or is denied passage, touring for as long as we can bear the splintering of our single entity transforming itself back into a multitude of molecules, cells, each microscopic particle flying off on its separate tour, destiny and destination.

Touring. One tour's ending. Goodbye to the dead one who seemed to be one of us and now isn't. Death creates a sudden stranger, makes the island more mysterious. The island turns a new page, we disappear. Does our traveling bring us any closer to understanding where we are, whose place this is, where its borders begin or end. Do we chant or pray or sing to pry secrets from the dead—clues, no matter how tiny, to help map the territory where our tours might lead. Do we hope the one whose visit here has just ended will pave the way, scatter some usable signs, some tangible proof the land has been walked before.

Inuit Eskimos build man-high heaps of rock to break the Arctic tundra's monotonous desolation. One of these cairns popping up against an empty horizon is the only sign of life a hunter may encounter for weeks. Will we find markers stacked and shaped, stones invested with the power to speak.

Like a shopping mall each night, the world busily cleans itself of all traces of our presence. The shopping mall, just as the city it serves, attempts to sustain an illusion of *tabula rasa* for the next day's visitors. Beneath the skin of appearances lies the machinery that not only scours surfaces but seduces us to forget that we see only what we're supposed to see; the shopper, the tourist feels real (pays top dollar) to the degree that the world is performed freshly for his or her consumption—as show, spectacle.

The world passes through the tourist. The tour consumes us, not vice versa. Always a step ahead or a step behind, the tourist is never there exactly, never sees or hears or smells or touches the country nor its inhabitants exactly, always experiences something other, something else—an illusion, an itinerary packaged, sold, administered like doses of a drug, unless, perhaps, we imagine a world in metaphors, making it up, making up ourselves as we travel, dream, tell stories.

29 DECEMBER 2000

In a little essay she's reading by Bruce Chatwin—who happens to be the author of *The Songlines,* one of my favorite travel narratives, a book whose words form a palpable landscape just as the aboriginal people he's describing construct from songs and myths the physical environment they inhabit—Katrine said Chatwin poses questions that had arisen on the climb to Ste.-Anne—what's wrong with being a tourist and why has touring earned such a bum rap. Her comments on his comments sparked the metaphysical excursions—being as touring, touring as being—la di da—I've set down here for better or worse and now I'm wondering if the author is a special case of tourist. One permitted to eavesdrop, gawk at a stranger's funeral without feeling like the worst kind of presumptuous meddler.

Are authors required by their trade to peek and pry, make presumptive strikes on other people's privacy. Are authors paid to be voyeurs. Expected to penetrate and violate boundaries defining personal space. Blur those boundaries, ignore them, explode them. Should authors operate on the premise that no one really owns anything. That the inner life, our ideas, emotions and imaginings, are common property and authors have right of access. Minds and bodies not granted to us, only leased, franchised. Space and time we occupy folds up behind us, disappears like the circus when it strikes its tents and leaves town, and since we're transients maybe we depend on authors and art, maybe we need them, desire them because we like it when we're reassured something happened, someone was there, a record survives.

Isn't the writer as troubadour, wandering minstrel, clown, blues singer, itinerant preacher, etc., a necessary and welcome exception or counterweight to assertions of ownership. Isn't territoriality—the emotional investment arising from the belief that you own a place, that you are a place's special darlings, that you and yours belong there and possess divine title and privileges—don't such presumptions trigger the turf wars that have plagued humankind forever. Doesn't the notion of territoriality (supernatural claims of owning property and places) inevitably bleed into the notion of owning people—whether you call it marriage, love, family, or slavery.

Does the traveling writer liberate space by not claiming it. Authentic touring. Passing through and asserting no prerogative, acknowledging by one's departure that one doesn't belong, never expected to be anything other than observer or passerby. Isn't it okay then to stop and join the mourners on the hill above Ste.-Anne. Why should anybody be offended by a stranger who brings nothing, takes away nothing. But is the author really so innocent. How does she or he differ from any other rude, crude trespasser on grief's privacy.

What if Katrine transformed herself into an invisible sprite like Ariel and flew around whispering into the mourners' ears, "Don't mind him, folks. He's a writer. He means no harm. Just ignore him. Go about your business as if he's not there."

Would she be telling the truth. And if so, what would it mean, what would it say about writers and writing. If I have no stake in what I'm seeing and writing, what's the point. Why should my words be trusted. How would they convince. If I'm not included in what I'm describing, what am I bringing to the scene besides the inevitable disturbance of recording it. What do I intend to take away after my visit, my tour. Why Martinique and not some other place. Does it matter. What's my connection. Yours. I think about the classic irony of a photojournalist with an expensive camera snapping pictures of a starving child. Why not barter the camera for food. Or smash it. Why hasn't the photo shoot been scuttled, broken down into as many immediate, life-sustaining acts a photographer and crew could squeeze out of their equipment, pockets, hearts. Does the writer as tourist earn an exemption in this sort of situation. Are we being reminded of the arbitrariness of values, beliefs, ethical standards, human and humane obligations. Reminded they belong to no one, no one owns them because just beyond the place where we are, other places lie, and things are different there.

Authors fragment themselves, shift ground, claim the only ground is shifting ground. Are such moves more than simple evasion of responsibility. Is there a naïveté, arrogance, madness peculiar to artists. Do they believe no reckoning occurs, no moment when the tour crashes and the calculated, cultivated distance between observer and observed collapses. Does the realm of values connecting the tourist to others exist like a view through the window of a passing train, there only when the traveler chooses to look.

I remember the blue men. In a scene from a movie a group of filmmakers, totally wrapped up in the tangle of their personal lives and the business of creating a film, are speeding across the desert in a Land Rover, music blaring, a joint circulating, the Sahara's vastness just another video to sample through the truck's windows when *"Pow!"* a coup rocks the Land Rover. Driver hits the brakes and the stunned occupants scramble out to discover a blue-robed boy lying dead in the sand. Nomads wearing blue robes like the boy's materialize from the apparent emptiness, surround the outsiders, impose upon them the brutal, implacable local law. Demand a life for the life taken.

We keep walking past the cemetery gate and descend into Ste.-Anne, stopping to let a boy and the bent old woman he guides cross in front of us. He steers her with a fingertip on her elbow, gingerly touching her sleeve as if he's afraid his dark skin might stain the many-buttoned, frilly white blouse blazing above a long black pleated skirt. In the mourners' eyes, are we dressed appropriately, John and Katrine, Katrine and John, in our white skin and black skin, her hand tucked under my arm.

30 December 2000

Traveling here below—a line from a gospel song I heard as a kid in Homewood AMEZ Church. On another occasion, night, returning from drinks at Leon's joint in the village of Ste.-Anne, a starry night above and below us as we stood on the hilltop, the lights of cottages, inns, hotels ranged along the deep curve of the bay created the illusion of a second sky full of constellations signifying not only the town's presence but its history, its myths represented by pinpricks of man-made stars piercing the veil of night, spangling the blackness of the invisible sea that must be there, isn't it, because you see it in daylight when you walk to or from Ste.-Anne, a noble vista advertised by the bureau of tourism plaque, dazzling sea and seamless blue sky shamelessly posed for consumption, but tonight's another occasion. Above us a thin, bright arc of moon like a line tracing the bottom curve of a woman's breast. Behind us, beneath us, the village beginning to close itself down—"evaporating," Katrine says.

Ste.-Anne's narrow streets lined by wooden row houses of two or three stories, reminiscent on a smaller, dilapidated scale of New Orleans' French Quarter with its intricate wrought-iron screens, railings, balconies, fire escapes, its elegant louvered windows and doors, *faux* openings painted or molded to preserve balance, symmetry, and proportion in each facade. Actual doors and windows enclosed within a decorative row of simulations so order and design rule even in these skimpy tropical replications. Versailles excess, extravagance, redundancy, refinement quoted and sampled in little houses framing Ste.-Anne's claustrophobic streets. Dating from the colonial period, the dwellings manifest the *béké's* elaborate dreams, the expertise of African artisans, dwellings seedy now, neglected, crumbling, paint peeling, interiors gutted, abandoned hives ceded to squatters, the descendants of slaves who built them.

Peeking in restaurants that occupy many of the better-preserved or restored colonial remnants, checking out prices in the boxed menus posted beside each restaurant's entrance, it's obvious that the old order of separate accommodations, separate fates for blacks and whites remains in force on Martinique. Apartheid effectively maintained by economic inequality and force of habit as it once was by Louis XIV's Code Noir statutes, guns, and whips. One quick glance inside a dining room confirms that this place for Europeans, that one for locals of African descent, the odd white face in a black crowd or beige one in places where whites gather only reinforcing the dominant pattern of division.

An *animation* in the town square, brown people in ole-timey costumes performing traditional dance and music for a predominantly European audience, does its frenzied, overhyped bit to express in a different medium what the black or white eating places proclaim: the unbroken stranglehold of the past, the indelible ink of the contract struck in Martinique nearly four centuries ago between Europe and Africa.

How bizarrely odd it is. How irresistibly heartbreaking and comic and hyperbolic and everlasting and impressive and sick and reductionist and thoroughgoing and tawdry and sentimental and inescapable and transparent and evil this keeping alive of what's never been alive, this Frankenstein animation of the good ole days, this replication—electronically magnified and projected on a portable stage in the village of Ste.-Anne—of a virtual reality created hundreds of years ago by all the crude technologies and ideologies that Europe could marshal in the 16th century to quicken its daydream of worldwide domination.

In a black bar where we sip our *rhum ancien* for a third of the price it costs in joints where whites congregate, almost every male wears a baseball cap pulled down tight on his skull, and 90 percent of the caps sport the Nike swoosh. Brown men (and men only) here, except Katrine and another woman, European looking, who sits with a beige guy near the front door. Leon, bartender and owner, one generation removed from Burkina Faso, plunks down a bottle, not single shots, on our table. An honor system based on mutual respect and trust determines the final accounting of how much you drank and how much you owe. Though we can't see the performance just around the corner in the flea market quarter of Ste.-Anne, the thumping bass of canned music driving the dancers rattles the boards of Leon's tiny *boîte* and we have to shout at each other to be heard above it.

Passing the stage, we'd stopped a minute to check out the action. A group of graceful, athletic brown dancers—the men costumed in white planter's white suits, the women in turbans matching their ankle-length, colorful, aproned dresses—swirled around a platform they shared with huge loudspeakers. A quick glimpse enough to tell me I certainly didn't want to stick around. Pulling Katrine by the arm, I didn't simply leave—I fled. No way could I enjoy the skill of the dancers without also feeling sorry for them, sorry for myself. Sorrow mixed with anger and frustration. That the performers might be very good-looking—and good at what they were doing—only made the situation worse. Why here. Why now in this particular setting, in a ring of people who didn't look like them, spectators anxious to clap and cheer, to be impressed, entertained, ready to reach in their pockets and pay, for all the wrong reasons, like the crowds drawn by brown, nomadic, acrobatic, hip-hopping, break-dancing squads in New York City subway stations.

31 December 2000

Once upon a time merchants negotiated the right to supply clothing for slaves laboring in Martinique's cane fields. The trade in slaves generated many similar collateral deals, establishing a far-flung network of profitable exchanges of goods and services, stimulating the accumulation of investment capital in Europe, instigating international cooperation (and terror), creating interdependencies and alliances (and ruthless, bloody competition) that became the foundation of today's integrated (and obscenely exploitive) global economy.

Quick fortunes could be squeezed from African flesh, and everybody wanted a piece of the action. In 1731, for instance, a group of businessmen from Vannes—a town in Bretagne just a few miles from the present home of Katrine's family—launched an "undertaking to go from Vannes, whence we were outfitted, to the coast of Guinea in the ship *Diligent* belonging to the brothers Billy and Mr. La Croix, our outfitters, and thence to Martinique to sell our blacks and make our return to Vannes."

Much has changed since such eager, small-scale forays into international trade, but certain prerogatives, certain unequal relationships persist. European merchants who won the right to dress slaves still dress the slaves' descendants in high-fashion Parisian knockoffs or Nike gear or plantation costumes for animations like the one I could hear but couldn't bear to watch or the tacky livery that brown women and men, working hard for a living in tourist hotels and restaurants, must wear to transform themselves into comforting simulacra of eighteenth-century servants, the hotel's bonded property *à votre service, mesdames et messieurs.*

You could say brown Martinicans have always been dressed to kill. Today's young people in hip-hop outfits, Tommy Hilfiger, Armani, Versace stuff, yesterday's lady's maids dolled up in silk to complement their mistresses' finery or female field hands naked and accessible to master under a coarse chemise or male slaves clad only in the minimalist afterthought of a loincloth as they're marched off to labor all day under a broiling tropical sun.

The franchise to dress also grants the power to undress, to stipulate in the name of economy or efficiency or style or identification or division or perversity or sexiness or morality which body parts are covered and which not. The colonist's prerogative to exhibit or conceal the native's body (oddly mirrored in the license to undress themselves and tourists from abroad that results in the ritualized look-but-don't-see nudity of Martinique's beaches, Euro-flesh displayed as if invisible to the gaze of natives who serve them) seems a legacy no one's in any hurry to modify. How else account for stripped brown bodies celebrated, flaunted, flashing in your face everywhere—billboards, TV ads, labels and logos, dolls, souvenir calendars, posters—public proof of who owns the native body and can bare it with impunity.

Behind the registration desk of our luxury hotel in a spot difficult to miss hangs a bas-relief decorative plaque. From a turquoise background a pretty, young, turbaned African woman greets guests, one chocolate breast coyly, completely exposed above the scooped neck of her peasant blouse.

Who let you out of the house, girl, dressed like that. Who told you to go round with your titty all hanging out. Who's your mama, child. Your daddy. You gon catch your death, girl, sashaying round half-naked, don't care how hot it seem. Whose grinning ho are you, my sweet sister. Whose gaze are you nailed up on the wall to please, to seize. Any old body. Me. Mine.

Who owns you, child. The hotel. Some old pomade-head *béké* planter. Any tourist who spots you first switching down the track. Is that you I see trapped in a mirror behind the desk clerk's shoulder. Or do I see a black hole. Girl, you ought to be ashamed of yourself. Ashamed of me, too, standing here gazing back at you. Pretending you're not there. Pretending I'm not here. Wondering if I'm eligible for your naked, provocative, come-on smile or leer or invitation, or are you just welcoming me, your gig to welcome anybody, everybody with a sweet, innocent invitation to paradise.

Who gets paid to plan and execute these seasonal dressed-up animations so dependent on ancient, damning alliances, allegiances, discredited assumptions, bankrupt partnerships. Who's still trying to convince me the dancers cavorting in their market-day best, big-house bought or borrowed or stolen or handed down, who says these are Martinique's mothers and fathers, my mother and father. Who believes this minstrel parody of old time servants' night off high-stepping and fetching—stepping on me and mine, fetching racist archetypes and stereotypes out of the island's closet. Who's sponsoring this ghost pageant in living color. Am I supposed to identify, see myself, my past, my ancestors' misery and fortitude and laughing-to-keep-from-crying anguish, my parents' and parents' parents' refusal to be smothered, to be stripped and flayed and disgraced and recycled as grinning clowns. Where in this spectacle am I supposed to find the pursuit of freedom, bloody resistance, any echo of the transcendent, miraculous determination of African people, their choice, in spite of kidnap, murder, torture, the withholding of language, education, economic opportunity, full citizenship—to be somebody, someday. A choice made in spite of the disinformation imposed by charades like the one in Ste.-Anne someone thinks is clever and cute and entertaining, the soap opera, coon show, gone-with-the-fucking-wind fantasy of the way things were.

Yes, my mom and pop danced. Taught the world a new language of dance with African alphabets of motion through which the body could articulate desire and dreams. They danced. I do. Yes. Dance a complex, demanding language in whose deep structure lies the rattling of chains, popping of whips, shouts and curses of sailors who herded African prisoners onto the decks of blackbird slavers to make sure the cargo's alive. Africans dazed by the stink, filth, heat, darkness of hours confined in the hold, swaying, stumbling, blinking, chained two-by-two, struggling to stay erect as the ship pitches and rolls. White nigger sailors cracking whips, playing their peasant ballads and chanteys on pipes, harmonicas, accordions, commanding the slaves to move faster, to hop, to shake, wiggle, and shimmy-wobble to keep our blood flowing, our juices vital. A few festive minutes in the sunshine, after we'd unsnapped ourselves from the dead or hopelessly sick and tossed those bad investments, that spoiled meat to the sharks.

I hear them splashing now. The waves. The bodies splashing in the splashing waves in the static and spit and feedback of a humongous sound system that belts out jumpy specters of quadrille and ballade. I shut out the syrupy melodies, imagine the music creolized by our stamina and wit, our flashing hands and feet, our chanting into unforgettable, lilting, honeyed, poisonous island songs, European forms stretched to accommodate

African rhythm, African gossip, African promises and curses and despair, negritude's drumbeat assurance and intelligence. Finger-popping, hip-shaking defiance stretching other people's music to fit ours, disciplining it to conform with the separate reality of our different cultures we brought across the Atlantic in our different bodies and different minds stored with different memories, different pantheons of spirits living and dead. And just as our bodies and minds reinterpret European music, European languages, we transform the grammar, redefine the lexicon of what Europeans attempt to say with their power to dress/undress us.

1 JANUARY 2001

The old year passes.

A tacky *prix-fixe* feast with questionable champagne last night all good because Katrine and I enjoyed the occasion together, dancing to zouk and salsa and soul and whatever else we caught in open-air cafés and clubs lining the path to the beach. By midnight just about everybody crowding the dance floor. Until then the mainly European patrons in this row of tourist joints content to sit at their tables, eating, talking, staring at each other. Katrine and I had started early, a bottle of chilled rosé, dancing with no company aside from the familiar beat of colored music welcoming us, making our bodies smile on our first forays, white woman, brown man, having fun, staging our own little mini-animation, our version of past/present/future, and for some reason I didn't feel shy, didn't mind the eyes, paid them no attention except once or twice wondering what they were thinking if they were paying any attention to the mixed couple breaking in the dance floor, the New Year.

Creolized bodies (and body language) transform the clothes Europeans sell them, dress them in, sell them in. Yesterday and today. The manner in which African-descended people (and their multinational imitators here on the island and everywhere else) wear their clothes is not unlike the way Martinique-born Patrick Chamoiseau, winner of France's most prestigious literary award *(Le Prix Goncourt),* transforms French. He invents a hybrid language, even plays creolizing tricks on Martinique's Creole (all's fair in love and war). Both Chamoiseau's prose and the innovative adaptations of imported clothing exhibit the strategies of Creole speech—imitation, parody, eclectic sampling, recycling the old, spontaneously improvising the new, layering meanings (multiple rhythms) to speak simultaneously to different layers of an audience. Brown flesh covered and uncovered like Christo dresses buildings (an entire island once) so what's beneath is problematized, recontextualized, accrues new meanings, stimulates an alternative vision that rescues the viewer from the usual unexamined scenery dutifully absorbed. Bodies dressed like the music that dresses the island, music borrowing Afro-Latin beats, disco remixes, country-and-western licks, appropriating European forms from folk to classic to pop, biting African vocal effects—falsetto, melisma, onomatopoeia. Zouk's daring, happy-sad *métissage,* quoting, blending, innovating—a hip-hop *Oh, Susanna, don' you cry for me* segues to the "Ode to Joy" from

Beethoven's Ninth Symphony rippling over the hotel's breakfast room one morning.

I'm sorry we didn't bump into more Creole dance and bodies on New Year's Eve, see more brown people styling out, profiling, clean for the holiday. What's the word in Creole for the African-American vernacular "clean," as in dapper, decked-out, sharp, hip, fine, looking good, dap, one of those connoisseurs who can dress down, dress up, redress, address, return to sender the clothing allotments imported from abroad. Brother so clean a stranger will say, *What's up, Money,* meaning, "You look good, my man, good as a walletful of clean, crisp bills." (Is there also buried in this good-time greeting a memory of the bad ole days when slaves, not allowed to possess money, accumulated clothing to serve as a medium of exchange.) *Clean* traditionally reserved for male dress, but it can apply to ladies as well, although the brothers' compliments to well-dressed women tend to be more sexualized, as much about body as what covers it. In spite of reductive fantasies of the male gaze, black or white, African-descended women have stayed *clean* since their harrowing arrival in the New World. As Joan Dayan points out in *Haiti, History, and the Gods,* slave women—compelled by law to dress plainly when walking public streets—stylized *plain* into a fashion statement influential in the court of Louis XVI.

Creolized styles of dress appear not just on holidays, Sundays, for dances and social gatherings. In the street, in school, at work, at play, Creole creativity intervenes—oversize and undersize garments, one pant leg rolled up, caps worn backward, pants so low on the hips that underwear or the cheeks and crack of the ass exposed, a new, rearguard décolletage. Prison and hospital garb sampled—no-lace shoes, no belts, drawstring pants, smocks stenciled with institutional numbers, initials. The white-bread look of Pendleton wool shirts or expensive yuppie garb synthesized with Bronx living larger than life, baggy drapery, flashes of gold, gangster luxuriousness, ostentation. No end to the art of redeploying, reinterpreting, subverting the clothing meant to impose and inscribe not only race, color, and class, but enforce a way of being.

Just as words are audible signs of a person's invisible, silent, interior mental universe, clothes embody ideas, literally dress thought. And since dress is a language, it bears the deadly weight of all communicative exchanges in the fossilized world that colonialism leaves behind. A people who have suffered the double whammy of enslavement and then colonization remain eternally unsafe, their lives at high risk, because in the eyes of those who once owned them, their only *raison d'être* is to serve. Or disappear.

A once-upon-a-time slaveholding, colonized society such as Martinique's never lives down its past as long as relations between the so-called "races" continue to express ancient patterns of one group's subjugation of the other. The names for an ex-slave may change—freeman, worker, colonial subject, citizen of France, nigger, native—and ex-slave owners may adopt different names—boss, *patron,* entrepreneur, capitalist—but all communication between descendants of masters and descendants of slaves remains haunted, stigmatized by the terms of the primal bargain that brought them together—the marketing of human flesh.

Even today, acts of speech between black and white recall the archetypal situation here on Martinique, when talk between Africa and Europe originally sprang up. Europeans in charge, barking orders, Africans compelled to submit, first to the domination of a foreign tongue, then to the fate that the unintelligible words prescribed: Work or die. After such a traumatizing introduction, would learning a European language by Africans ever be innocent or neutral.

Because African languages did not count as speech to European ears, the African's mind appeared to his captors as strikingly naked as the African's body. During the process of seasoning—the boot camp where newly arrived slaves were quickly, brutally conditioned to submit to the rule of serve or die—Africans learned a few words and phrases and were provisioned with a few scanty articles of clothing along with instructions on where and when to wear them so as not to offend the master's notions of modesty or decorum.

Forced to abandon African words, African attire, the captive population assumes the language and dress codes enforced by the master, but at the same time Africans begin a long, subversive campaign to maintain within themselves a separate reality. At the core of this alternative way of seeing the world are concepts and beliefs transported from the Old World. Inward resistance counteracts outward submission. *Take low* we used to say in the Homewood streets. Sometimes you just got to take low. Absorb an ass-kicking, stay down on the ground today so you get your shit together, come out fighting another day. Spirit work. Rope-a-dope. Playing possum. Doubleness. Multiple selves. Secret selves. Preserving an inner sanctuary, a reality no one can touch or alter. Privacy, independence, an internalized counterculture based on African traditions, organized to relieve the pressures of living as an oppressed, despised class. *Silence, cunning, exile* the formula articulated by James Joyce, a survival strategy useful not only for Irish peasants but the ancient practice of serfs in Russia, serfs in Bretagne, the Hebrew children in Egypt, the Wretched of the Earth across town, across the globe.

Is it possible to survive in a highly structured, oppressive environment—a slave state, a colony, a prison, the army, a convent, a boarding school, a boardroom, mental hospitals, today's carceral, globalized consumer culture—without succumbing to the definition of being that such hermetically sealed, "total" institutions (as Irving Goffmann labeled them in his 1961 *Asylums*) inflict upon their inmates. How is it possible to resist the enormous pressure to conform—the constant, premeditated assaults designed to destroy individuality, self-determination, self-worth, self-esteem of mind and body. Or ignore seductive, coercive rewards for submission.

How can captives forced to behave as slaves not become slaves. Creolization is a positive response to this conundrum.

For some captives acculturation to the ways of the West must have started in the slaving factories along Africa's west coast, but it intensified dramatically, ruthlessly once Africans disembarked upon New World islands such as Martinique. Creolization is a particular process of acculturation rooted in language but not limited to language behavior. Creole languages, according to prevailing linguistic theories, begin as pidgins—ephemeral, primitive, oral media of exchange created by people who don't understand one another's languages. (Is it silly to suggest love begins as a pidgin, too, in fumbling, frustration, the need to understand and be understood by a mysterious other, a visceral language powered by desire, communicating with eyes, gestures, grunts, touch when words won't do the trick.) From its humble start as a pidgin a Creole gradually elaborates itself until it becomes a fully fledged language with rules of grammar, syntax, a lexicon, taught to children as a first language and able to perform the complex work of communication as well as Dutch, Urdu, Russian, Egbo, French.

Given the necessity of accommodating themselves to the tyranny of European speech, dress, etc., Africans devised strategies (I'm calling the process creolization) to resist total cultural domination. Through a variety of techniques, Africans disciplined themselves to gain some personal control in their dealing with their masters.

All languages systematically discriminate by privileging certain sounds (phonemes) to form words and meaning. This privileging imposes order on the chaos of sound, but an order ultimately circular and arbitrary, culturally specific, culturally bound. Every language attempts to make sense of the world, sense that also exerts control over the world, sense serving the language bearers' agendas and desires, self-serving sense to name and structure reality. Martinique's Creole challenges and contests the sounds and meaning of French, destabilizing the logic of privilege and discrimination that speaking "proper" French authorizes.

Whether it's a single person speaking or the systematic creation of a parallel language to compete with French for linguistic hegemony of the island, creolization depends on play. On the imperfect fit, for better or worse, between humans and the institutions they create. On gaps, breaks, discontinuities, incongruities, plain human orneriness, irascibility, irrationality, undependability, unpredictability, stupidity, and the passion for not telling the truth.

One way is never the only way. If chaos doesn't exactly rule the world, chaos makes sure no word is the last word of any debate. Play on. Not even death gets the last word. Creolization summons ghosts, revenants, turnabouts, hails the reversals, the topsy-turvy of carnival. Creolization evokes the possibility always to undo and redo and come undone. Creole cultures and speech preserve the possibility of choice—even if your fate's decided, you can always imagine ways to refuse it. So what if the opportunity to refuse explicitly never comes? Conjure up the fun of busting up the master plan. Keep the dynamite fuses growing out of your skull dry. Who knows for sure what's going to come next. Next, the perpetual invitation and challenge on playground hoop courts.

In the Gauguin Museum just outside Le Carbet, I saw a wineglass from some St.-Pierre *béké's* table. It had survived Mount Pelée's devastating 1902 eruption, and smeared, elongated, scorched, its original tint exploded so it appears tie-dyed, a piece of stemware twisted almost but not quite beyond recognition, displayed in a glass case with a new identity as a curiosity produced by natural disaster, and then I saw it again, months later, in a catalogue of surrealism, featured as a piece of sculpture, an object of art and desire.

"O my body, make of me always a man who questions!" Frantz Fanon, born in Martinique in 1925, ends his classic deconstruction of colonialism and race, *Black Skin, White Masks,* with the above wish. In the same book, he asks directly the question posed implicitly by Creole language and culture: "Should one postulate a type for human reality and describe its psychic modalities only through deviations from it, or should one not rather strive unremittingly for a concrete and ever-new understanding of man." As he develops his analysis of a new being to replace both colonizer and colonized, Fanon's performance is often pure Creole in its irony, wit, bricolage, anger, mimicry, wisdom, brutal honesty, its ambivalence toward authority. Whether the authority of "black" or "white," "Africa" or "Europe." Fanon's nascent, decolonized, de-raced individuals, like Nietzsche's ideal artist, must undergo metamorphosis: first a cleansing to become open like a child, then conscious assumption of the burden and lessons of the past, and finally roar and struggle to challenge the past and prepare a better future. The last shall be first, the first last. "The dialectic that brings necessity into the foundation of my freedom drives me out of myself," wrote Fanon. "It shatters my unreflected position."

When slaves believe they are powerless, they become complicit in their servitude. Creolization begins here, resisting slavery's most evil effect—self-destruction.

Creolization means taking nothing for granted. In the case of Martinique, it means not accepting the authority of French (the island's official language). Creolization works like elegy—lyrically summoning what's absent and desired. It is skeptical, it peers into cracks, despises easy answers, attacks language, undermines, revitalizes, reroutes, personalizes words. Creolization is an ongoing process of renaming. Like good poetry it perpetuates between words and meaning, sound and sense a state of tension, unease, competition, dissonance, irony. Keeps old wounds alive, not because suffering ennobles, but because wounds hurt and creolization wants to insure wounds don't close before healing's complete.

Creolization insists on the moment, the fresh start each moment offers. Since the past is always present anyway, creolization foregrounds the immediacy, urgency, and drama of daily exchanges with other people. Such encounters constitute the unfolding narrative of a life, the temporary *stages* upon which people speak their piece, their mind, name names, negotiate the meaning of names. Creolization as an attitude toward experience says, Let's start here, now, in this present moment that is no less than an intersection of past and future, a crossroads where folks going different directions can meet, running water, where we can't set down our feet twice in the same spot, a place haunted by old forms, old habits, old rules, old gods clamoring as always for us to follow their lead.

Creolized speech or dress, like the multiple rhythms of African dance, music, or fabric open multiple channels of meaning. Tying knots in a headcloth, varying the tone or rhythm of a word delivers multiple messages simultaneously. Cued by stylized modulations of sound or movement—*different strokes for different folks*—layered creolized utterances play to and construct a layered audience. The reply a tourist hears from a waitress is not necessarily what is understood by her nephew, the busboy who's also working the tourist's table. Depending upon degree of familiarity with the speaker's (performer's) culture, people in an audience are able to decipher a portion, large or small, of the encoded meaning.

Consider the chaos of a news broadcast on the television screen: an announcer's face and voice-over, sidebars, inset videos, the crawl of factoids, ticker-tape bulletins flashing, intermittent displays of logos, ads, call letters, etc. Now imagine integrating all that mess into what seems like a single coherent message while at the same time preserving the reams of info on the screen so that each message reaches a targeted segment of the audience without excessively distracting or disturbing other viewers. That's something like the art creolization strives to master. Preserving choice. Focus on one without sacrificing the many. And vice versa. Multiple presences, many possibilities available with minimal static and interference.

Dress, music, speech, dance, all modes of culture can be creolized—that is, consciously constructed to reflect and participate in an ongoing struggle over the nature of reality. Unfortunately, neither side in the struggle is prepared to acknowledge the other side's words as a point of departure for describing, let alone resolving, the conflict. You could say this stalemate, this mutual unintelligibility constitutes the struggle. Before a storyteller begins her tale, before she decides when and where it should commence, who should be included or excluded, who are its villains or heroes, victims or abusers, she must choose a language—French, Arabic, Hebrew, English, Creole, Tajik—and all languages come loaded down with names, with a history of naming names, a record of who's right and wrong, of winning and losing, far from neutral.

In the context of struggle over the nature of reality, African descendants' bodies don't simply endure passively, they are engaged actively, like music and dress, in creolization. Obviously there's the rainbow palette of skin colors riffing, signifying on European complexions, on the European fantasy of *white* or *black.* And beneath the skin the body's physical mass of flesh, bone, blood also mutates the clothing that Europeans would dress/undress us in. The truth of our suffering, our witness, our degradations and triumphs produced corded arms, high, round butts, manual laborers' massive shoulders and thick trunks, slim legs, the ball of muscle high on the shank of people run around, running around, running away. Part biologically determined difference inherited from African phenotypes, but mostly a record of labor, turmoil, accommodation, flight, the adjustments and adaptations over many generations to soul and body consuming tasks like murderous sugarcane cultivation. Africa-descended bodies shaped by New World experiences, bodies streamlined, syncretized, intense, expressive as crackling Creole speech. Bodies endangered as they evolve, just as speech is endangered. As the official language of French usurps a larger and larger share of the island's discourse, Martinican writer Edward Glissant warns that Creole will erode and become "in its day-to-day application … increasingly the language of neurosis. Screamed speech becomes knotted into contorted speech, into the language of frustration."

Yet Creole speech retains a hole card—silence. The silence of refusal. Refusal in the extreme case of Africans leaping from the decks of slave ships, letting the roiling waves seal their lips. Or the less drastic refusal that André Breton includes as part of a trinity—*the gift of song, the capacity for refusal, the power of extraordinary transmutation*—comprising the common denominators of exceptional poetry: "Poetry worthy of its name is measured by the degree of abstention, of refusal it implies, and that negative component of its nature must be maintained as essential: it balks at tolerating anything already used except when diverting it from its previous function."

From those first moments of existential nakedness in the New World, African bodies attuned themselves to hearing silence, a silence full of signs, the silence that drowns and transcends words. Africans parsed silence, interpreted and exploited it. The silences rhythming our music, the responsive, listening silence of call-and-response, the primal, echoing space between drumbeats, heartbeats. The silence of waiting—waiting powerless and frustrated for commands, news, food, clothing, a turn in clinic lines, waiting for a job, peace, freedom, for an opportunity to speak back to the others who seem privileged eternally to dole out the necessities we wait for.

Bodies silently kneeling and praying to silent, ancestral gods. The lyric pause of silence when spokes of sunlight penetrate the clouds or the night sky rains stars and you realize you can silently steal away, step for a quiet instant into a place elsewhere, away from what seems to be the unceasing tumult of an *administered* life of toil and trouble.

Silence as a counterpoint, counterweight to the fugue of many voices, many languages buzzing imperiously, incomprehensibly around you. Silence as an answer. A rejoinder to chaos. Deep, contemplative silence words can't touch or explain or represent when you're walking through a cane field or along an urban sidewalk with others and their words then their voices fade away, give way to what's unspoken but churning inside you, and that motion—the one-of-a-kind, wordless, primal language only you understand—itself dies away to stillness and quiet as you submit to the abiding presence of silence, silence words never relieve, never break, the strangeness of being a tourist, a wanderer in Babylon whose body divides in a fashion that words can't describe, except words pop up anyway, and you slip away to sit beside the waters and dream of Zion. And right on cue, believe it or not, the morning I sit in a hotel in Ste.-Anne writing the sentence before this one, Bob Marley's version of "Rivers of Babylon" begins smoozing from stereo speakers hung in the corners of the dining room: "How can we sing King Alpha's song in a strange land?"

"They know how to make even the fetters of slavery serve them for adornments," wrote Lafcadio Hearn. Consider the headrag, aka headcloth, headkerchief, headdress, mammyrag, turban, etc. The cloth Europeans imported to the Antilles mainly from India, England's colonial gold mine where cotton could be grown, woven, and dyed cheaply by a captive labor force, madras cloth intended to hide African hair, sanitize, render less offensive its difference, conceal its attractions, to streamline, reduce, make uniform, stifle the individuality human beings might express when they own their hair and can wear it as they choose.

This early European project of human modification collided with an entrenched African tradition of elaborate hairdressing, hairstyling, hair wrapping. The planters' treatment of African hair as a questionable substance—to be ignored, kept out of sight, out of the way when slaves cooked in kitchens or served in dining rooms or cleaned the master's toilets or bedrooms or slept in master's bed—created a site of contestation and resistance.

African women sabotaged the purpose of the clothing allotment by subverting instructions for its use. Altered the headcloth's form and function. Rag or smothering hood becomes turban, a decorative wrap whose expressive possibilities evolve over time, irresistibly, given African resources of ingenuity and dexterity, the spirit of captive women determined to unknot the puzzle of the rag, undo its humiliation, unlock the cell that's supposed to incarcerate and thereby eliminate the allure of a woman's hair. The obliterating sack is untied, retied, disciplined, taught to speak, to sing Creole.

Oléane, the brown lady who cleans our room, 436 Bequia, Ste.-Anne, Martinique, and sweeps the balcony on which I sit each morning to write these notes, gave me a speech lesson. Her fourteen-year-old daughter, who studies English in school, supplied the translation below of phrases in French describing Creole hair-wrapping practices, phrases printed on a souvenir postcard Oléane used to refresh her memory, then handed to me a couple of days after I'd asked her about the *pointes* or *bouts* that Martinican women tie in their *têtes*—the colorful, scarflike cloths covering their hair.

LES DIFFÉRENTES TÊTES ET LEUR SIGNIFICATION
(The different headdresses and their meaning)

Tête 1 bout: Mon coeur est libre
(My heart is free)

Tête 2 bouts: Mon coeur est engagé, mais vous pouvez tenter votre chance
(My heart is spoken for, but you can try your luck)

Tête 3 bouts: Mon coeur est pris
(My heart is taken)

Tête 4 bouts: Il y a de la place pour qui le desire
(Everyone who tries is welcome)

Tête chaudière: coiffure de cérémonie
(Ceremony headdress)

Whether hidden or exposed, disguised or highlighted by cloth, hair is, from a biological perspective, just a special adaptation of skin. Hair provides one more instance of how European license to dress/undress Africans extends its hegemony to the body's most intimate, last/first line of defense. Skin is the primal boundary defining a person, separating inside from outside, self from other, the interface where individual identity begins and ends. Skin also functions as a container, literally keeps a person in his or her place. For the colonist setting out to construct a two-tiered, master-and-slave, apartheid society in the New World, the darkness of African skin must have seemed a heaven-sent blessing, a ready and waiting sign that would divide ruler from ruled. Problem is that on island outposts of empire such as Martinique the inevitable sex between Europeans and Africans reveals very quickly the impermanence, permeability, mutability, and unreliability of skin color as a marker of race. To solve this problem the settler drapes everybody in a mandatory second skin: *black* or *white.* Though invisible, this covering effectively overrides appearance. Not to acknowledge it risks severe punishment—isolation, exile, torture, fines, death, prison, ostracism—within the colonial order. What you might see when you look at a person (or yourself) is replaced by what you must see. The colonial solution goes further, ascribes value to this imaginary either/or. A hierarchy with black at bottom, white at top, and gradations of gray in between cancels the Martinican skin color, the colors Lafcadio Hearn rhapsodizes:

> A population fantastic, astonishing—a population of the Arabian Nights ... many-colored ... all the hues characterizing *mulâtresse capresse griffe quarteronne métisse chabine* ... it is only with fruit-colors that many of these skin tints can be correctly compared ... there are banana tints, lemon tones, orange hues, with sometimes such a mingling of ruddiness as in the pink ripening of a mango. *(Two Years in the French West Indies)*

In the identity and status games played on the island, black or white trump all other colors and/or qualities of character. By renaming skin color, the settler seizes control of Martinique's story. In the settler's Manichean vision, color (stipulated as black or white) and race are simply opposite sides of the same coin. History is rewritten. Racial division survives unaltered by hundreds of years of sexual encounters between Europeans and Africans. In spite of the contrary evidence in front of our eyes, it's as if the encounters never occurred. Certainly never occurred if we search for radical shifts in the balance of power and privilege such prolonged, intimate exchange might have produced. Race and color as read by the settler nullify the past. As for the future, the settler's color blindness empowers him to proclaim, no matter what colors you think you see, that those kids over there playing in the sand are black—and, therefore, can never become true masters of the island.

Like mandatory head wrapping, coloring all people black or white imposes an extra skin. This artificial, invisible coloring serves to naturalize brutal colonial interventions. Like the yellow Star of David, the South African or Palestinian pass card, the issuing of an official skin color regulates unavoidable intercourse between warring parties. On the island, skin color is supposed to tell you where people fit and *why.* No further explanations necessary, if you believe the hype, if you ignore the violence of rape, murder, economic oppression required to socially construct the blackness inflicted upon ex-slaves of all colors.

2 January 2001

Why does Martinique take me back. Way, way back to ancient, dark places. Isle of *revenants,* of ghosts, of rugged mountains and dense forests depicted in Creole folklore, the turf of monsters, of zombies, of wicked Père Labat, of fabled shape-shifting creatures who exit their lairs at nightfall, lying in ambush at crossroads, beside cemeteries, in the shadows, insatiably hungry for prey and devilish play. Why does everyday life on the island—especially in urban areas such as Fort-de-France, with its stores, malls, monuments, plazas, traffic jams, billboards—feel like a huge animation, a low-budget, fraying-at-the-edges production, people and places dressed up to look like Paris or New York as a little Paris or New York might be imagined by somebody who's never visited those cities. Why are people walking around perfectly content, it seems, in this thin-skinned, wannabe replica of an original that doesn't exist. Why so many pharmacies. Why do downtown streets empty early each evening.

Martinican Edward Glissant speaks of "a web of nothingness in which [Martinique] is ensnared." Famous European visitors have also commented on the island's aura of insubstantiality. In 1941, on his way to voluntary exile in the United States—and, by chance, to discovering Aimé Césaire and the poetry of "negritude"—André Breton, artist and theorist of surrealism, said of Fort-de-France, "The city itself was adrift, deprived as it were of essential parts. Shops, and everything in their windows, took on a disquieting, abstract character."

Anthropologist Claude Lévi-Strauss, another French intellectual fleeing the too, too solid reality of a Nazi-controlled Europe, and soon to collide with the fascist Vichy officials who governed Martinique during much of World War II, notes: "At two o'clock in the afternoon, Fort-de-France was a dead town: it was impossible to believe that anyone lived in the ramshackle buildings which bordered the long marketplace planted with palm trees and overrun with weeds, and which was more like a stretch of waste ground with, in its middle, an apparently forgotten statue, green with neglect, of Josephine Fascher de la Pagerie, later known as Joséphine de Beauharnais." Of course equal time could be granted to more favorable impressions of Fort-de-France and Martinique, native and tourist views, but at the risk of quoting him too much I want to register

Lévi-Strauss' thought that Martinique's unfinished or temporary or decaying or transparent quality in Western eyes may have something to do with the fact that "the first thing we see as we travel round the world is our own filth, thrown in the face of mankind."

I imagine myself naked, chained, sick, standing helpless before a person whose language I don't speak, who doesn't speak mine, a person who's kidnapped and transported me an immeasurable distance from my home, a person whose stare tells me nothing about his plans for me, except I know because I've been his prisoner for months that he's capable of extreme cruelty and brutality, that he beats, rapes, tortures, that during a seemingly endless voyage across the sea he tossed the weak, diseased, and dying overboard, and know in his eyes I am not a human being like him but a beast, an animal without name, family, country, or voice, I'm his property, a *thing,* disposable, replaceable as he sees fit.

At that ground-zero, bottom-line moment, truly existential since I'm stripped of all props, all illusions my society and culture have supplied to buttress an identity, I stand alone, nothing, no one, as emptied of meaning as the void I'm dangling over, the void of those eyes fixing me in a stare, eyes (are they blue, blue as Katrine's, blue as these Martinique skies) deciding to pass me to the right or left, deciding whether I live or die.

Here on the island, I feel closer to that raw moment. Why is it so viscerally present. Is it simply because I'm a stranger, a tourist and Martinique a kind of funny money. You know how that goes. Though francs (euros now) function here just like dollars function back in the good ole U. S. of A., the French bills and coins don't look right, don't automatically assume the authority of the money I'm used to. The bricks and boards, the highways, the landscape and sounds and smells of the island are missing something. Certain markers are absent, certain indications of substance and depth. To accept my material surroundings requires a willed suspension of disbelief and I'm not necessarily prepared, nor in a hurry to expend the effort. I'm cautious. Very cautious. How much faith should I invest in what I see around me. What lives inside the things that appear to be everyday, ordinary stuff here. What would happen to me if I settled into this world. Whose face, whose voice, whose eyes await me at the bottom of this island's make-believe. Whose stare would fix me. Determine my fate.

I have to remind myself continually that Martinique is indeed a legitimate substitute for the environment I'm used to, that it possesses value, that I'm not being conned by a counterfeit, a stage set I can see around, see through, a mock reality that might dissolve any instant. The feeling's not entirely new. Dread dogged me even within the walls of houses I grew up in. My first year of college, one of seven or eight brown faces among thousands of white faces, I experienced moments when all the ivy-covered university buildings, the walled gardens, tree-lined paths, the entire placid green island squeezed into the middle of black, urban West Philadelphia became as slippery as a daydream. Classrooms, cafeterias, libraries had nothing to do with me, and I expected them to vanish, wished they would vanish, since they offered me no shelter. No welcome. No hiding place. I hated never knowing what the hell might happen next. Would they run me off. Eat me. Crown me king.

Maybe because I'm not firmly ensconced in Martinique's man-made, physical presence, it's easier to lose my place in time. I'm not convinced I'm anywhere, so I float everywhere, from scene to scene, backward and forward in time, and what surrounds me floats too, changing shape, conspiring with my moods, unshackling itself, freeing me. Because seas surround it, there are luscious views everywhere at the edges of Martinique, offering a panorama of shimmering possibilities immense beyond imagining, but the sea also mirrors the mind's restless tossing and turning. Sea the site of madness and ships of fools and ancient, constant peril, where reason can be drowned by its own ceaseless turbulence.

3 January 2001

The sound of tropical rain storms is dense and thorough. They come and go quickly in Martinique. Soaking, saturating in minutes. Sometimes there's the warning of frenzied palm fronds rustling, whipped till their sighing is indistinguishable from the sound of a torrential downpour. You can't hear exactly when one segues into the other. Or a drenching shower can glide in stealthily, blue sky still visible through slants of rain, the brief deluge arriving swift and silent as darkness drops on the land each evening. (Some—among them Martinican novelist Raphael Confiant—claim darkness *rises* here.)

At dawn I heard what I guessed was the bellowing of one of the ghost-colored long-horned African cattle that graze the scrufty hillsides behind the hotel. Then screams. Human or a cat's high-pitched, passionate caterwauling that sounds so human when cats thrash and fuck and moan like human lovers driven to lick and paw and hiss and howl at each other like cats, but none of the above really because the sounds fracturing the morning stillness resonated from the lungs of some creature larger than a cat, larger than a man, a bull-size something with the deep, muscled chest required to amplify the eerie cries puncturing my sleep and jolting me up in bed, cries acting as a cue for the intense quivering of the coconut palms to commence, the keening, soughing rattle of their swaying caresses of one another and themselves, each drooping frond stirred wide awake, rippling like a flag in the wind, a long-fingered peacock's tail whose feathering tips tickle the fishbone spines of fronds close to it, stroking, rubbing, fiddle-bowing till the whole tree's agitated, shuddering, the frantic motion synched to peak when the first huge drops of rain plummet from the sky, drum against the red-tile roof.

But I'm losing the order of the sounds as I try to reconstruct it. My desire to tell a story chases away what happened. I lose ground faster and faster as more happens. Other sounds are heard, imagined, recalled. They interfere, spoiling my attempt to retrieve what came first, second, third. One sound does not neatly follow the next, nor conspire with the next, nor produce the next. I'm losing the experience by attempting to recover it.

Writing is a forgetting, a technique for abandoning things, leaving things out, replacing with the artifice of narrative what's happening or what's already gone on about its mysterious business. All experience dissolves into chaos and terror if we remember too much. No beginnings, middles, or ends. You never can be sure where you've been, where you are, what's coming next, unless writing fixes the problem. Or pretends to fix it, pretends the world stands still long enough for words to form and catch up.

A bit later, after rousing myself and checking the weather through the shutters, in the time it took to fix a cup of coffee on the outdoor stove behind our room, tiptoe back past the bed where Katrine's asleep, slip outside again and settle down in my balcony chair, a rainbow had formed, arching from a snowy bank of clouds to another that's dingier, grayer, shaded by the dark mass passing above it that probably had ferried the earlier shower and now gloomed half the sky a smoky, purplish gray, the kind of moisture-laden cloud that could creep in and loose tons of rain, a circus clown sneaking up and dumping a bucket of water over the ringmaster's unsuspecting head.

Like the cascade of sounds washing over me earlier, the rainbow had simply appeared, not there when I first checked the sky, but there now, surprising me, no warning, no logic, no plan, just there, its radiant bands of color intensifying as I watch.

Maybe I'd dreamed the cries. Maybe memories, dreams, reality indistinguishable in the fog of drifting awake. Or maybe I still wasn't awake yet, and to cut through this muddle, I looked up again at the sky. In the place where the rainbow had been on fire, only an unbroken screen of gray. I recalled the sculptor Giacometti's frustration: how the model disappears, he said, each time he looks away to check his copy of it. A different model when his eyes return.

In about a week we'll be returning to a country greeting the new millennium with a new (and very probably illegally elected) cracker president to replace an outgoing Southern prez, a country that celebrates a third, Thomas Jefferson, on its two-dollar bill. Thanks to a dedicated band of ruthlessly aggressive, insatiably greedy thieves who are systematically plundering the nation's resources, any two-dollar bill cached in my passport case will probably be worth about a buck by the time I get back to the States, and nothing else about my country's official good-ole-boy, backslapping, back-turning address to a new century pleases me, either. No doubt, with a rigid, mean-spirited, not very bright or imaginative, bought-and-paid-for executive at the helm, things will be getting much worse before they get better, especially for the people (mine) to whom the new leader feels no obligation except trash talk to keep them running in place.

Poor, stupid me. All these Southern presidents keep me confused and running. Who won the Civil War. Until an editor told me otherwise, I thought Jefferson adorned twenty-dollar bills. Huh-uh. It's another Southern prez, Andrew Jackson. But the face on the twenty-dollar bill is close to that of the mythical Jefferson we've been taught to adore. Floating hair *(beware, beware)* surrounds a visage that could be Keats or Shelley, an icon painted by one of Browning's enraptured pre-Raphaelite circle. The leader represented as an intense, ethereal dreamer, thinker, visionary with the broad (read alabaster) brow, the poise of a god.

Jefferson's sweet talk about democracy his most enduring public legacy. Monticello his monument. Jefferson remembered for a golden pen that inked in mellifluous, memorable, eighteenth-century prose an Enlightenment view of humanity's sanguine prospects, even when Anglo-Saxon inheritors of Greek and Roman civilization find themselves a precarious

3,500 miles across an ocean from Europe. Jefferson's words a blueprint for a society never seen before in the Old World, a spunky, spanking-new dispensation for a virgin land, a society in which all men will be treated under the law as if they were created equal and endowed by their maker with certain inalienable rights, these and other fundamental principles enshrined in a written Constitution and Bill of Rights that Jefferson co-authored, promising all those who would dedicate themselves to participating in this novel experiment in democracy an equal opportunity to work and prosper and secure happiness in a stable, righteous state. Or something like that I seem to remember from what I was taught about my country's birth.

The image of Jefferson on the two-dollar bill commemorates his role as a noble founding father, ignores his career as slave master. Why not a five-dollar bill with Massa Tom kissing Sally Hemmings, his beige mistress, behind the barn. Why only the good side. Isn't Jefferson's complexity, the continuing ambiguity of our national legacy, worth commemorating. Are we supposed to forget—like we're supposed to forget the new president's troubling credentials, his lack of distinction—that Jefferson's dream for a new nation is among other things a sugar-coated riff on the same ole, same ole European power trip of conquest and exploitation, theft and enslavement, a plan for transforming the tropical isles of the New World into cash cows for investors, demi-paradises where white men who choose to settle would be re-enthroned as masters of Eden, top dogs in the chain of being, reigning over the rest of creation. Islands ripped off from the original inhabitants, their descendants dead, exiled, or eternally enslaved, more dark help imported when necessary, more Calibans visibly, viscerally, body and soul at your service *messieurs, mesdames.*

After a tour of Monticello organized by my hosts at the University of Virginia as a special treat—a tour led, coincidentally, by one of my former MFA students at UMass who'd relocated from Massachusetts to Virginia and become a professional guide—I wished for a truckload of dynamite to blow the place up (no harm of course, David, to you, you conducted a fine tour and were quite gracious—I'm imagining a reverse-neutron-bomb wipeout not harming a hair on your head or anybody else's). The few Monticello items worth saving, not much really from my (admittedly antagonistic and not very patient or discerning under the circumstances of my tour) point of view. I noticed mostly unprepossessing, sentimental bric-a-brac or website memorabilia, poor copies, imitations, Euro-trash fashionable in Monticello's heyday. Who'd miss it, except collectors/investors with a financial stake in that particular species of stuff. Would the world be a poorer place without it. Is the world a poorer place when lives of the poor are sacrificed every moment for the greater good of the precious few able to indulge themselves with the commodities on view at Monticello, commodities they can own and display to substantiate their pretensions to a higher, more refined, reserved sphere of living.

Who would lose if Jefferson's house on the hill were utterly erased. Don't many of the monuments we preserve encourage people to yearn for the good-ole days, not renounce, not regret, nor swear *never again* to these days neither good nor old. Forgetting the past would be exceedingly dangerous, yes, but because the past stays alive in one fashion or another, forgetting it is also impossible, so the issue is how to remember, what to remember, how to save and cherish the complexity, the ambiguity and mixed messages we dare not forget. (Okay, maybe we just drape Monticello in a mourning pall, not blow it up.)

Not that we'll ever achieve the clean slate of a least-common-denominator past—a version of our history not pleasing anyone but offending nobody either. That would be just another way of forgetting, creating a Disneyland, an illusory Eden, starting over clean and innocent. But who decides finally whether a Confederate flag should fly over the capitol building of South Carolina or be enclosed in a glass case in a museum or buried in a time capsule—or torched? Who decides when a monument to Frantz Fanon should replace the oft-defaced statue of Napoleon's consort Joséphine de Beauharnais in Fort-de-France.

Should the brutal excesses of the Marquis de Sade's *One Thousand Days of Sodom* be expunged from the literary record or ostracized as pornography or studied as a mad, brilliant, prophetic enjambment of the daily crimes—rape, torture, flogging, dismemberment, murder—perpetrated during the end of the eighteenth century in France's Caribbean sugar colonies with the crimes enacted upon the bodies of poor servant girls that an aristocrat holds captive in his château outside Paris. And speaking of de Sade, is his notion to return to sender the psychic waste that France was dumping in the Antilles more or less commendable than Tom Jefferson's bright idea for disposing of surplus African-Americans by exporting them to die in the sinkhole of Haiti. Doesn't de Sade's frighteningly logical, perverse conflation of two realms, two moral universes—an enlightened mainland France with its barbaric colonies—expose the bloody contradictions, entertained by Jefferson, that predict the terror in France and Haiti, the genocidal slaughter of racial "others" scarring the twentieth century.

Absolutely destroying every remnant, sowing salt in the Earth so nothing would ever grow or prosper where Monticello once stood felt like a proper, final solution the afternoon of my visit, but maybe now I'd prefer ruins, physical, tangible proof of what had once existed on the hilltop site that Jefferson carefully chose for its combination of isolation and domination, invisibility and arrogant, Las-Vegas-neon-sign advertising of himself. Scattered rubble would be a record of outrage, of redemptive violence responding to one man's megalomaniacal flaunting of himself, his kind, as above, as better than those he claims the prerogative to rule and oppress. Gaping foundations, demolished shells of wall would be a monument dramatizing the extreme measures the downtrodden must exercise to rid themselves of continuing abasement, poisonous, institutionalized insults to their intelligence and dignity. Why tolerate monstrosities such as Monticello that are lingering symbolic representations and celebrations of the divine right of masters over slaves. Jefferson got too much all wrong, totally ass-backward when he imagined and then erected Monticello. Why are we still giving him credit today for noble enterprise and intentions.

But wouldn't tearing down Monticello be like burning the Library at Alexandria or knocking down giant, ancient Buddhas in Afghanistan or stripping kidnapped Africans of their culture or burning synagogues. Yes and no. I don't know. Each case is different, inextricable from the chaos of history contextualizing it. I do know life must make way for death and death for life and on and on, and I know some hero's always trying to call the tune, name the tune for this dance. Cultures have figured out many ways of honoring their dead, preserving their ancestors' memory, integrating old wisdom into the present, and lots of these methods don't depend on fetishizing material remains. As a national monument to celebrate a man, a spirit, a heritage, Monticello feels partly like an over-the-top tomb, more like being in the presence of a zombie—one of those walking, talking undead still stalking Martinique's mountains and woods long after the creature should have been decently buried.

Compared with the Grand Anse of Martinique, Monticello is *Beverly Hillbillies* tacky, a mishmash of architectural styles, undigested and competing tastes, featuring low-grade practical Yankee ingenuity in the service of some cockeyed notion of how one's betters live. Faux European elegance, Europhilic pretensions streamlined, updated with the latest eighteenth-century high-tech gadgetry to simulate and adapt Old World style and comfort in the wilderness of North America. It seems that Jefferson envisioned Monticello as a kind of ultimate pleasure palace and laboratory for a retired philosopher-king, a self-sufficient estate that could be wound up, turned on, and run itself—much like the clockwork universe of the deist god that Jefferson worshiped, a computerized, digital superhouse coming soon to your nearby gated community.

The juice powering Jefferson's home on the range, little house on the prairie, big house on the hill was African slave labor. Slaves invisible as electricity, slaves in cellars, behind screens, false doors, slaves toiling in fields, residing in huts cleverly landscaped to be invisible from the master's windows. Monticello honeycombed with subterranean chambers, tunnels and galleries, niches under terraces, cut into walls. Sally Hemmings' bed hidden in a box disguised to appear as a canopy over Jefferson's bed so she can descend from it at night like a dark, ministering angel when Jefferson desires her company. Slaves buried in boxes waving palm-frond fans.

I wonder how a humanistic philosopher concerned with theorizing the rights and dignity of individuals experienced the contradictions between what he preached and practiced. Scholars (see, for instance, Richard Hofstadter's seminal essay) have catalogued the ambiguities and ambivalences in Jefferson's copious writing, but that doesn't exactly answer my question about how it felt, what it meant to him, Jefferson's attempt to live simultaneously in domains as separate as Enlightenment Paris and Martinique, a whitened America and one besotted by slavery. How would he have responded to seeing these realms yoked in de Sade's parables of lust and domination, his fantasies of bodies as toys, dolls, commodities, bodies stripped of clothes, subjectivity, humans treated as replaceable, disposable as farm animals. Two domains—one loftily abstract, theoretical, the other a worldly, corrupt, ruthless pursuit of selfish ends. Domains antagonistic, explosively contradictory, theory versus practice, flesh versus prosthesis, real versus virtual, two versions of life Jefferson imagined he could join seamlessly at the hip.

Of course one reason I'm probing Jefferson's sentiments is because the problem hasn't gone away. For much of my life an honorary white-guy status has been granted to me, and the benefits have been enormous. The costs as well. What does it mean for me to be touring Martinique. Where am I. Where do I stand.

Jefferson, the self-absorbed, obsessed, cynical, Faustian, comic overreacher, realized in the grand structure of Monticello (and facilitated with his cunning inventions) a Prospero-like veil of illusion and trickery. A virtualized reality with clonelike slaves his Calibans and Ariels. An everyday existence administered so it excluded the ugly sight of human bondage. African servants apparently had disappeared, though they continued to labor round the clock for the master's benefit and pleasure. A domain collapsing public and private, black and white, true and false, have and have-not, power and powerlessness, dream and substance into one thoroughgoing, perpetual, seamless whole. Jefferson's estate, the Martinican plantation owner, me, you propped up by the lies, brutal violence, and selfishness of an ideology (capitalism's pseudo-Darwinian survival of the fittest) calling down to those who serve our needs, whose backs support the pulpit upon which we stand and shout, "Hey, I got mine! Nobody's fault but your own, my friend, if you don't get busy and grab yours!"

Jefferson the philosopher-king living in splendid isolation in his hilltop mansion, apparently independent, apparently innocent, apparently free of responsibility and unholy desire, living in a prosperity apparently without end, amen. In other words the state of being, the immunity from consequences of selfishness that candidate Bush promised his fellow Americans during the last presidential campaign. The promised land a majority (almost) of American voters endorsed when they chose candidate Bush in an election that was a remarkable example of Jeffersonian empty rhetoric and sleight-of-hand, simulation and substitution. Woe is us. The election a sham contest between two essentially indistinguishable parties that engaged in petty squabbling to obscure the absence of serious debate. The predictable results: the reinscription of complacency, false security, an all's-well-that-ends-well, one-step-forward-three-steps-back consensus. We're all Americans in this soup together, aren't we, as united as the fingers of a hand in a fist when fists are necessary, as separate and different as those same fingers when it comes to what each receives as a fair share of bounties and privileges. Rich and poor, colored and white, master and slave, all the hip-hopping, Puffed-up Daddies and Don King Trumps and Madonnas and Michaels and Britneys and Rockefellers and J.Los and Jane Does and just plain Joes coexisting, equally inseparable, separately unequal, one big happy *us* against the world.

4 JANUARY 2001

A virgin land. Martinique's stunning beauty belies the history of kidnap, murder, forced labor, rape, incarceration, destruction of minds and bodies. How could this land harbor any history—skies and water so blue, hills green, fields fruitful, meadows bedecked with wildflowers—when it appears so transparently pristine, eager, clean, so innocent of wear and tear, a river of sensuous delights, impossible to step into the same spot twice, and even if history lurks here, why should we care, why bother to acknowledge it since the island presents daily, immediately, no questions asked, no forced marches through a dark, horrendous past—the bright, untampered sunshine of a new day, new water, a moving feast, a malleable dreamscape wherein anything is possible, anything permitted for the tourist lucky enough to reach its shores. This new island like a new lover's arms.

Part of the business of preserving the past is denying the past. Historical synecdoche: substituting a part for the whole. Rewriting indeterminacy. History's complex fugue of past, present, and future represented by words as linear narrative, as metaphor, as sign. Imagining Eden also imagines erasing the past. Postulating, dreaming the existence of a moment when time begins is a denial of the vast, seething depths upon whose surface the bubble of any Eden floats, until it pops. Like old European theories of separate creations to explain differences among races, the idea of a New World Eden rationalizes and forgives moral contradictions of the Old World.

Here on the island illusion reigns. You begin to believe you can pull the plug on time, let the endless waters drain away. Achieve stillness, stasis, insularity. Each day a *tabula rasa,* an empty cup set before the tourist: Coffee, tea, or rum, sir? Rejuvenation, forgiveness, boundless potential, a chance to fall in love again with your mate, yourself, all included in the round-trip fare. The island is getaway, timeout, time between, vacation, *vacances,* vacancy, an alibi. You're excused, you're literally *elsewhere.* And if the island serves us so, why not. Should it, could it be more. Or otherwise. For whom. How. When.

We talked the second half of the night away with the sweat of the first half drying on our bodies, just the two of us, two of us, Katrine and John whispering so as not to disturb our neighbors through the thin wall our rooms shared, neighbors from Marseilles we'd already treated to the feral zouk of our love-making, gasps grunts yips sighs yelps smothered and subdued as much as possible, yet irresistible, taking over in spite of holding back for the neighbors' benefit, the bed slats rattling, bodies smacking like waves in the *bâteau-ivre* cruise of the night's first half.

I'm a man who will be sixty on my next birthday. Too old for certain kinds of foolishness, but here I am, enjoying all-nighters, loving the chance to push past the past, welcoming all I've ever been back into the mix, welcoming excess, silliness, the body ridden till it drops, the mind excited and desire still revving up the senses, so I sit up in bed and chatter with Katrine about nothing, anything, Eden, eternity, R. Kelly, Bretagne's weather, Shakespeare's *Tempest,* the color of her eyes, Thai food, and for a moment it's all exceedingly important—sexy, urgent things it seemed you'd always wanted to say or hear and you just know the one beside you feels the same, pumped up as you are by letting go, not kids again, but for the moment, for the time being you're stealing, stretching, spinning out of your body's pleasure, hunger, and exhaustion a high that might not ever end. Not young again, not any particular age—you're what you've experienced before on rare occasions, both good and bad, you're all ages at once.

The sorcerer in his pointy hat and billowing purple robes waves his wand and through the twisting mist appears an enchanted island. Each life an island floating in the sea. Here on Martinique we're tempted to forget for a while that each island possesses its unforgettable history, the past (whether we choose to read it or ignore it) indelibly inscribed in its features, its sounds, the barely perceptible pulse of engines animating the present tense of its sensuous moments, the *éblouissance* of its changing weather. Each life distinct and often opaque even to the gaze around which it forms, the subject that the gaze creates a visitor, a tourist of itself, losing as much ground as it gains, the gaze temporal, temporary, mortal—the island disappearing at a slightly slower rate than it appears, materializing from the mist, but disappearances always gaining on the speed of appearances until inevitably the two lines meet, cross, and nothing else appears or disappears. I'm trying to imagine that instant but it's not me, not yet, so I can't. No more than it will imagine me after the lines converge.

And love. The island named Katrine. The island named John. Is it true that the more time we spend together, the less time there is remaining for our love. Love as zero sum. Eating itself to stay alive. How do you figure the odds. Time gained, time lost and why bother to calculate, why waste one second on speculating how long love will last. Why tamper. Why wait.

5 JANUARY 2001

Day off.

6 January 2001

Goats tip, saunter, prance, spritely on their tippy-hooves with an arrogance and superiority untouched by the knowledge they're going to wind up in a spicy curry—like pretty young girls or little kids—goats are kids, too, aren't they—anyway, that's how goats trotted and stopped just before they reached the end of their tethers at the edge of a country road in Martinique.

In St.-Pierre on May 22, 1848, slaves riot after the unjust arrest of one of them whose name comes down to us as Romain. They had been promised emancipation as soon as the boat bearing the slavery-abolishing decree arrived in Martinique from Paris. Frightened by riots spreading across the island, the colonial government was compelled to act. When the Paris packet docked, there were no slaves on the island. What a difference a few days make.

Shakespeare's *Tempest* is, among other things, a prison narrative, a melancholy reminder of how long the European colonial project has lasted, imprisoning first the colonized and then the colonizer. Everybody's life a cell on wheels—it goes wherever you go, says *The Tempest's* anti-touring story—you can run but you can't hide. Everybody's locked up. Even Prospero, who seems to carry all the keys in his deep pockets, Prospero who owns Caliban and Ariel, who rules and claims he owns the island, who orchestrates the delusions of the Venetian aristocrats he holds captive, even Prospero is incarcerated by his plot to right wrongs, restore equilibrium, justice, exact vengeance for what he believes is his unjust exile on a tropical prison island.

The Tempest is also a prescient vision of the contemporary muddle—how movement is being replaced by virtual movement—going anywhere, everywhere without leaving your living-room couch, without paying dues. Going nowhere, the sentimental wish for experience without the risk of acting, for nostalgia without suffering a past.

The go-go guy twangs his magic twanger and we're off. On the fabulous running-in-place tour, the virtual excursion, to an island that can be Kathmandu, Lima, Paris, Martinique, or any or all of the above. Reliable as Disneyland's pocketful of here, there, and everywhere pavilions. Mohammed doesn't have to trek to the mountain, the mountain comes to his tent. In a cave the Twin Towers flicker on, flicker off. You ante up the price of the ticket and your destination's guaranteed as good as gold, if you believe, if you kick back, relax, close your eyes. In an instant you're there. Far, far away. The Old World staged in the New World, the New World staged in the Old so nobody has to risk traveling, risk crossing unknown seas (there be Dragons). Let the guy with the magic joystick and full-color brochures or your friendly Travelocity lady transport you, Froggy, beam you up, Scotty. Everywhere is anywhere and everything is anything and if you don't exactly understand what the fuck that means, here, take two of these, the big, round greenies. You'll feel better in the morning, my son. When you awaken on the island.

Shakespeare's miraculous creation forecasts the modern imprisonment of all of us in somebody else's self-serving story, each lonely, distinct one of us trapped, enraptured, a performer in a globalized, virtual, administered show. To participate in this spectacle that seems to offer collective security, collective access to the necessities of life—air, water, food, space—we must sacrifice difference: the difference defining our sense of self, the difference defining others. To survive we must settle for a narrow, prescribed range of possible selves, and of possible others, settle for difference that confines rather than liberates who we might become.

"The only people for me are the mad ones," wrote Kerouac, "the ones who never yawn, or say a commonplace thing, but burn, burn, burn."

While some of us are content to go along with the show, to sit still and voyage everywhere courtesy of the sorcerer's wand, more and more people are losing control of their lives. Movement (migration)—the traditional means human beings employ to save and/or better themselves—isn't working. Millions upon millions driven to move, to flee the place once called home, are discovering there's nowhere to go. They're surplus people—permanent refugees. The poor herded into camps, ghettos, confined at internment centers, homeless, helpless, destitute, the psychologically or philosophically alienated, beset by despair and anger in the midst of plenty. More and more of us each day are propelled by political upheaval, social and cultural breakdown, predatory economic practices into a no-man's land that threatens to outgrow the "First World's" fragile, temporary zones of safety and immunity, destabilizing, swallowing them like the sea takes back the land.

Prospero plucks shipwrecked passengers from the sea. Erases the past from their minds. His band of refugees repatriated into a country of dreams, a brave new world, or rather into the grand dream, grand scheme that serves Prospero's purposes. Until he removes the scales from their eyes, the stranded folk are enchanted, entertained by the magician's illusions as we are by contemporary illusions of self-improvement, self-control, self-determination in our economic, erotic, and political lives. Drugs and booze, the lies of advertising, the news media's deterioration into for-hire entertainment and propaganda, the exaggerated promises of science and technology, the dumbing-down of cultural, educational, political institutions have turned us back toward unexamined superstitions, back into believers of myth. The myth we can get up and go as we please. The myth that our world has devised a democratic middle ground, a relatively safe harbor for the majority of us where rich and poor, black and white, powerful and powerless, can peacefully coexist. The myth of progress, that change equals amelioration. The myth that no Prospero exists behind the scenes, paring his fingernails, arranging our lives to fit his controlling vision. The myths of fundamentalism acknowledging a god within the machine, *our God* and *only ours* and all power to him.

"Where is it safe to go as an American?" complains a Silicon Valley marketing consultant in *The New York Times.* "The world may have gotten smaller, but I can't go there anymore."

Lost at sea the Ancient Mariner moans, "Water, water, everywhere, / Nor any drop to drink." Tours, tours, everywhere, nor any place to go. Every place fast becoming the same place. The project of globalizing commerce, the forces that have conspired to shrink the world, to digitize, miniaturize, clone, and sell the difference of lands *outre-mer,* steal their resources, exploit their citizens have rendered most countries increasingly alike, unfit for their inhabitants and quite dangerous for tourists. Even the stay-at-homes who tour virtually risk life and limb going to the store around the block for a loaf of bread.

And then there's love. The love of Miranda for Horatio and Caliban for Miranda on Prospero's island, love that sometimes, in spite of the odds, seems to find a way, even among tourists and refugees, those two opposed yet strangely complementary roles embodying the basic human desire to move, to travel, to be other, to do better, desires more urgent and compelling in the current environment of ethnic and religious distrust, hate, warfare.

The worldwide project to control difference, to subject difference like everything else in our lives to the logic and demands of superheated international commerce must bear copious responsibility for the current deterioration of the quality of life. For superheated, Mount-Pelée-like eruptions of destruction and death. The irrationality and dangerous overreaching of the project are displayed as it simultaneously flees and seeks difference, establishes and abolishes difference, punishes and rewards difference, ultimately mandating a flat-lined zero, zero, zero of sameness, of redundancy and false equivalences.

If you can't be with the one you love / Love the one you're with / Love the one you're with / Love the one you're with / Dit dit dit dit dit dit dih dit / Dih dih dit / Dih dih dit.

So we spend the night making love and talking about the madness of the world and wondering what love might be and how it fits with the craziness, wondering why love touches us, stamps us, deserts us, why it fascinates and frustrates, leaves us cold, alone, and grieving, then springs on us again like the brightness of the life-giving Martinique sun when it seems to promise blue morning after blue morning forever after. The doing, the dreaming, two different worlds expressing two orders of experience, and the charm of the island or its curse, the power to reverse, to remove the opposition—vapory dreams of the present moment verify our flesh and the solid flesh of the past melts away. Our bodies are attuned to a song of constant meshing and exchange, doing and dreaming woven together until, finally, is there any difference here. The island's spell cancels the gap, the difference between what is and what we wish, between one self and other selves, between self and other, seducing, seduced, confounding us into submission.

With the edge terminally blurred between dream and doing, between what is and what's desired, between real and virtual, the island, all of it, feels outside time, a free space—a proposition to be seriously entertained or not, according to our inclination, the power of our will. What can we construct here. What can we get away with. This is the island's fatal attraction: its promise to give us the power to forget, the power to fabricate an existence free of contamination or intervention from our intimate personal and collective history, that secret package of terrors we're accustomed to carrying around like a second skin when we consider who we are.

Of course the island's promise to deliver us from the baggage of our identity can't be honored. The brief interludes when we believe otherwise are doomed to crash, pop like Eden, one more bubble in a flow with no beginning or ending. Here where we find ourselves now, always, is where we must reside as long as we're able to believe in the ghostly dimensions of our bodies, as long as our feet can solve the problem of walking on ground insubstantial as water.

7 January 2001

Silently revising yesterday's spiel is this morning's spiel. Not many new words added, all the old ones questioned. Writing erasing itself. But not quite. Like desire. Some mornings nothing fresh can present itself until old business, if not settled, is at least further clarified. Put on a different footing. Put away. A different foot put forward. The writing interrogated.

Is this a way of saying we come to the island to shed our illusions. Or it could be a way of saying we are what our illusions shed. Though each passing day shrinks the time remaining on our tour, each day also presents more tour. And less.

What registers some mornings as an almost musical, swaying whisper (like the body's first bemused stirring from a long, deep sleep) can also be a racket, wind through the palm fronds rattling like Venetian blinds, like ancient louvered doors and windows, clacking, chattering teeth each time they're opened or shut.

8 January 2001

The beach at Salines, opposite Le Table du Diable, the Devil's Table. One of the best days in the sun. We decided to spend the day there instead of scooting around the island in the rental car. The Museum of the History of Cane (where we'd learn that French colonial planters, forbidden by law to whiten the sugar they'd grown—how could darkness be the source of light—were required to export it brown and unbleached to the mother country, where it could be transmuted into the white, pure sweetener Europe was willing to pay for with its soul) could wait till Tuesday. We need some down time, a break—*boo-hoo, pity the poor, exhausted tourists*—from the rigors of vacation. Our rhythm, our choices feel right so far, even though the goal we'd set ourselves—familiarity with the island—has become an ever-receding horizon as tasks and obligations mount and the jobs we do get around to are often accomplished in a half-ass, cursory, last-minute fashion. In spite of inefficiency we seem to be achieving progress, progress not costing an arm and a leg of the bodies whose pleasure turns out to be the best reason to come to Martinique. Our bodies the key to the story, bodies upon which the island's able to practice its best tricks—water and sun, soft starlit nights, the caressing wind.

Almost obscene to complain under such beguiling circumstances, and setting aside a day of rest not a complaint after all, more like celebration of what the island offers, an opportunity to anoint a day to recover from all the voluntary excess and extremism of indulging ourselves in the beauty of consuming our days any way we wish, and our wishes mostly enticing us (after my dawn-to-late-morning scribbling) to pleasure each other in bed till one o'clock or so and then head for one nearby, gorgeous beach or another for sun and reading, then a late lunch of *poulet grillé, crudités, pommes frites* with a glass of *rosé frais* in one of the small seaside stands, then more water and sun, back to the room at five or six to the aftermath of a day gorging on the island's heavy-handed sensuality that builds keyed-up expectation in your body even when you're full to bursting.

Changes in air, in light, the sounds and smells of evening falling (rising) say there's more, always more, say that the tired ache of every body part is also an itch, a provocation waiting to be attended. You've been sated, laying for hours beside the sea in the tropical sun or an oasis of shade. You're a lush ripened fruit, almost spoiled rotten by pampering, teasing. Manhandled, penetrated, irrigated, grown round and full and prime, energy depleted to manufacture juice and pulp and dark, eye-shaped seeds, the magical husk of baked skin that seals raw, pink flesh and also allows the flesh to sip moisture through its pores, through the million openings of its downy, microscopic follicles that are licked by light, rain, breath, skin binding the fruit, protecting it, then thinning till it's ready to burst.

A long day in the sun can turn you into something like that so when night drops and you drop sleepy across the bed, heavy, slightly bruised, close to ruined, you're also playful, definitely not finished with the day, though you may desire nothing more than to be consumed, to be taken by a hand or mouth imagining you are its last sweet, salty supper even as you imagine yourself, will yourself to reach out for the mouth eating you and forget you're the fruit and tired and you sprout new digits, a mouth, a hunger of your own recovered, renewed, and try to gobble up the other whose lips are closing round you, whose teeth pierce you like the sunlight piercing in a thousand places the orange sarong wrapping Katrine on the walk to the beach, the other beside you in bed infiltrating the veil of your skin, both of you feasting, gliding through gauzy transparencies of difference, wearing and stripping them, blending skin, flesh, your separate dreamings, love's crowded, shared space, a single garment you both wear at the same time.

9 January 2001

Yesterday early in the morning from the balcony I heard our neighbors grumbling and fussing, the unhappy jostle of rousting themselves up and out to be on time for a day of guided touring. A glass-bottomed boat to spy on the fishes. A *rhumerie.* Botanical gardens. Part of the package they'd paid for, so no way were they going to miss the excursion. I couldn't really tell whether they were discussing the day's itinerary or one already consumed or options on the next day's menu. A middle-aged worker and family from the *métropole* on vacation, a very successfully employed, privileged worker who can afford the steep airfare from France and the price of food and accommodations on the island. Much grousing beginning their day, the same complaints and bad vibes you'd probably hear if you eavesdropped on their flat or tidy house in Marseilles, Paris, Toulouse.

Calling itself play, the packaged tour surreptitiously, perversely replicates the compulsory routines of working for a living, patterns so deeply ingrained they're invisible to the bearer, yet organize and discipline his or her everyday address to the world. Patterns repeated until they seem normal, correct, natural, the *only* way to live a life. Straight as a slanted world seems to a person doomed to walk crooked. Work for most of us a specific kind of activity—butcher, baker, computer-chip maker—and also a set of conditioned responses to time, a conversion of time to minutes, hours, days, months, years—clock time, calendar time internalized, linear, materialized time that overdetermines behavior. A dramatically reductive experience of time, a fiction that governs reality, like the fiction of race following us wherever we go.

Time organized in service of efficient production, distribution, consumption, our lives chopped into segments corresponding to the logic of a job, how the job fits into the grand systole and diastole of commerce. Like slaves on the sugarcane plantations of Martinique, my neighbors and I are caught up in an administered existence depriving us of significant choices about the most basic ingredients of life—the air, food, water we consume—and how we occupy the prime-time hours of awareness—when we eat, sleep, screw, travel, what we wear. Instead of the plantation's hard-core incarceration, we're constrained (and contained) by an illusion of freedom. Freedom defined as a prescribed range of choices—the chance to select from 105 TV channels, the chance to pick from an array of commodities portrayed seductively A to Z in a continuous rush of advertisements surrounding us 24/7, cradle to grave, the unfolding menu of goodies whose contemporary sign (accomplice) is the Internet's endless surfability, its apparently inexhaustible smorgasbord of virtual delights, if you don't mind that all 105 channels are shopping channels or that the net fishes for you. On the one hand mesmerizing choice, on the other hand a closed circle—a lonely, stark dependence on the owner and programmer of the apparatus, the technology producing the spectacle/carnival of choices. On closer inspection, the cornucopia of choice observed on the screen exists nowhere but within the machine's electronic digitized circuits. What you see is related to what you get in more or less the same way the ten-million-dollar lottery prize relates to each ticket sold to win it.

The slave's first choice to submit or die, and if life's chosen then the slave's rewarded with a deal: choices stipulated by the master. So much labor, so much pain will earn you this much fatback and greens. Christianity taught slaves to look toward heaven, that garden of delightful choices, for the ultimate reward of their labor. To convince the contemporary worker he's not a slave, to distinguish his lot from a slave's, he's promised a paradise on Earth, a mediated paradise in the domestic setting, the jackpot of exotic tours to a paradise across the sea, gratifications less delayed, more visceral than the slave was promised but just as dependent on acceptance of the package deal—on choice preempted. Choice dismantled and reassembled as specific quid pro quo compensation for doing the right thing. The master's version of the right thing, of course, the master's tit for tat terms, his version of a bargain, his choice of what constitutes your range of options after you've discharged your primal duties and obligations—the package deal. Five days or ten days. Or twenty-five years. Or life.

On the plantation a few days a year in fat seasons slaves were feasted and fed rum, allowed to dress up in the master's cast-off finery, dance, sing, fornicate with carnival abandon, encouraged (ordered) by the boss's Club Med smirking, indulgent cheerleading to act fools, stuff themselves, get high, recover their animal appetites, have fun. Our neighbors from Marseilles are privileged, wealthy, loyal, and lucky, yet also bullied by timetables, by somebody else's idea of pleasure, of time, of who they are, what they want.

The guided tour, itself a commodity, commodifies my jet-lagged, bickering neighbors. They sign on for the happy tropics and enter an assembly line, streamlined, efficient, and after their allotted days in the sun, roll out tanned and exhausted, ready, maybe grateful, for a return to the sanity of work. Grateful to be relieved of the burden of filling *free* time with choice A, B, or C so time doesn't just pass, pass away, become dead time, no bang for the buck it cost you. When the tour's over it's really just beginning since the next step is to recycle it into the routine of work, tell your fellow workers the story of the dream trip, the fish growing larger with each telling. Home again, home again, and you can transform any hangover of anxiety about the tour, process the glitches, the stunned, dazed somnambulism of your five- or ten-day getaway into what you thought you were paying for, what you believed you wanted. The tan, the snapshots, slides and videos, funny anecdotes, the sights consumed live that most people see only on postcards or TV or travel posters, this retelling, reconstituting, this ticket back as much a part of the packaged tour as the tickets you picked up from the airline counter at Charles de Gaulle. The hype must be perpetuated for those who would follow you to the island. You don't want to seem like a party pooper, do you. You don't want people to think you missed having a good time. So you spin your tale and keep the master narrative circulating. You don't reveal the dirty secret: The packaged tour doesn't transport you elsewhere. You stay on the job. It's your doubles who receive time off—cloned selves, cloned identities flying off on virtual tours.

As dupes of a packaged tour going nowhere, we experience the pervasiveness, the galling, frustrating, dangerous, ancient, stubborn lies of race that fuel this crossing-over that's not crossing, this coming and going that's standing still, this running away that's also running toward, this sneaking back and forth and denial and false starts, false ends, false Edens, purgatories, utopias, dystopias, this mess so intimately personal and also the rationale of institutions within and relationships among great nation states: the racialized vision of ourselves and our future, blighting the prospects of both. The paradigms of race lead to the same dead end Kafka visualized: the all-encompassing horror of bureaucracy spawning more bureaucracy until individual autonomy withers, human beings become cogs who keep the wheels spinning.

When the tourist arrives on the island the native must disappear. (And vice versa, as Fanon understood.) Since the island is given as a prize to the lucky, diligent worker, the native must stand aside, make no claims; the prize includes the native's space, color, prerogatives, identity. The tourist expects to enjoy the island unencumbered by those who've been displaced, replaced. What's the tour if not a golden opportunity to go native. The native population is superfluous, insubstantial as shadows cast by tourists going about the business of play. Shadows. Shadows who serve. Shadows. The stuff of darkness. Darkness denied. Darkness also sought, since the darkness of the other (or freedom from self) is what draws the tourist to the island. The tourist's desire to be other, to play native. The elusive darkness of what's forbidden except in dreams. Forbidden to anybody born with the responsibility of whiteness, anybody born eligible for the prize of the island. That kind of darkness can't be owned, only borrowed or imposed. A dark closet you can't come out of even though you disguise yourself for the duration of the tour in costumes the closet contains. The first shall be last, the last first—violent reversal (to quote Fanon again) the only way to free darkness, the only way darkness can free. And that truth echoes like the island's church bells on Sunday morning. *Ding-dong. Ding-dong.* Either/or. Black or white. Dark naked skin, dark native talk, music, food, dance, dress, no matter how temporarily convincing, no matter how much you pay to rent it, display it, the darkness not yours, not you. You made it all up. It disappears when the native disappears. When you appear.

Tourists flee to the island to become its natives, to escape the censorship of civilization, its discontents, its limits, its priorities—free, free at last. Free as the native, as natives living an administered existence to serve tourists. Free as natives fleeing, first chance they get, to the *métropole.*

Native lives are dangerous. So be careful. Crossing over no simple matter. Native life a reversal in the worst, negative sense. Natives endure a problematic status—soulless, nationless, savages, pagans, slaves, beasts. Crossing over to the darker side means defrocking your identity. You relinquish privilege. Natives possess no rights a white man is required to honor. Not healthy to venture too far into the heart's darkness. *Beware, beware, the Gulf of Benin / Few come out, many go in.* So take my hand. Let me guide you. Let me entertain you, says your precious tour leader.

The package tour excludes as judiciously as it includes. You are protected from certain risks and consequences of reversing roles. Remember Mistah Kurtz. Let the guide save you from yourself. Complete reversibility, complete exchange would be fatal. Fatal darkness from which there is no return. You can confiscate the native's dark skin only if he dies and sheds it—he can inhabit your pale skin only if you've surrendered the ghostly life filling it. Between you and disaster stands the tour bus, the Air France 757 flying you across the Atlantic to Martinique and back. Round-trip guaranteed, part of the package. The tan fades, momentary indiscretions forgiven or forgotten.

Beware. On the island natives dream of becoming you as lustily as you dream of becoming them. They say they don't desire to be you, say they just want what you have. However, being you seems to be the only means available for attaining what you possess. Color, because it's subject to change, to sun and miscegenation, becomes a problematic sign. Once desire strips away the official second skin of black or white, you can't depend on color to get you back home, nor keep the island's natives in their place. Who's the beige woman sitting at the table next to yours in a Ste.-Anne bar. What is she and what is he, the one whose tan hand she's squeezing. Who works in the cage next to yours at the bank back in Marseilles. Wow. Unless someone's in charge, it's sneaky-easy to get away with pretending what you aren't. The other. You. The magical island tour provides sunscreen and condoms to control pernicious, unscheduled exchanges. The package deal includes these accessories, but above all, it assures the tourist that Prospero's magic wand will dissolve all confusions in the blink of an eye. *Poof.* Everything's back to normal, to the way it was before you crossed the sea. The way you want it. Clear. Black and white. Native and tourist. Substance and shadow. Or so it seems.

Black people chasing whiteness. Whites chasing blackness. Same old jokes. Strokes. In the back of your mind where it's jammed to overload with stuff you think about, worry about, but can't talk about, you're wishing you could laugh off the whole silly mess.

Pretty fucked up when you get right down to the nitty-gritty chaos of these African/European exchanges. How long. How long. Martinique a place to escape to. Martinique a place to escape *from.* So what's the island. Where is it. Why all the fuss. The comings and goings. People paying with their labor, their time and lives for the privilege of touring another's life. Whites touring blackness. Blacks touring whiteness. A trip nowhere to where they've been all along. Neither black nor white. Each island of self, of difference floating in the same sea. A sea within. Where the search for difference, for freedom begins.

10 JANUARY 2001

That shrill, agonized screaming again. Is it an ineradicable echo of the conch shell each dawn summoning workers to deadly cane fields. Or does some primeval combat rage at night and what I hear the groan and bellow of the wounded, sprawled on the battlefield, not dead yet but dying, their cries a last protest against the rising light exposing their open wounds. Or is the screaming a sound track of nightmares amplified through the horns of ghost-colored African cattle bitten by tsetse flies in their sleep. A woman next door up to pee hears the screams, too, and asks no one in particular, asks way too loud for the hour—*Qu'est-ce que c'est?*—then imitates the eerie sound almost perfectly, catching its ratcheting peaks and valleys right on, the mewling outrage precisely miniaturized.

The tour's inside us. My neighbors. Me. You. Inside each one of us. The great bamboozling project of our times is to convince us the action's elsewhere, in a place or person we can't reach without the mediation of some self-appointed guide, expert, leader, prescription. We're being coerced into forgetting *You got to go there to know there.* The primary experience of our own bodies, our light is being devalued. Knowledge must be officially accredited and sanctioned to count. You go to somebody who *knows there* and they'll tell you everything you need to know about *there*—for a price. The price a radical reduction of what it means to live a life, own a life.

The packaged, guided tour—like many other highly profitable contemporary businesses—sells its customers something they already possess. The pharmaceutical industry is a prime example. But some such enterprises are even more virtual than drug companies. No factory, no material product required. What's sold is a mesmerizing rap persuading clients they lack and need what the business offers: more rap, more guidance. Need it desperately. The packaged tour sells clients access to difference. The scam works because it's part of a totalizing system that dispossesses. Guided tours, slavery, the urge toward conformity arise from the ruins: One order subdues and plunders another. Sells stolen goods back to the victim. Always exacting a terrible price, an extortionate rate of exchange. From the ashes no phoenix ascends. Only imperial eagles, circling birds of prey and vultures.

Slaves and tourists. The guided tour and slavery. After pointing out a few odd parallels, wouldn't it be silly, maybe even perverse, to push the similarities very far. Aren't slaves and tourists at opposite poles of the scale of privilege and freedom. As markers defining such a scale, however, both demonstrate how the initial, uncorrected error of racism permeates an entire social system and distorts its values from top to bottom.

A kidnapped African possessed the freedom of choice all human beings inherit at birth and retain till death. The range of choices perceived, the will and opportunity to pursue them constitute the adventure of anybody's life. Freedom is an inescapable condition and privilege of being, but the crushing weight of slavery can dull the spirit's awareness of its choices. It's not difficult to empathize with slaves who visualized freedom not as a metaphysical burden and privilege, but as the instant when body-consuming, soul-crushing labor ceases. And from the slave's perspective, wouldn't it be natural to conceive some master on the ground or god in the sky as the one to command this work stoppage, orchestrate the Great-getting-up-morning when you don't have to get up and trudge to the fields, when trumpets blow, thunder rolls, stars fall, the moon drips blood. Nor is it difficult to understand how the slave's vision of freedom perpetuates slavery by locating the key to freedom in the wrong hands. Like the tour locates difference in the wrong place *elsewhere,* in someone not the tourist.

Waiting for freedom to be staged as a spectacular animation in the sweet by-and-by (or waiting for a just society or waiting for a tour to deliver the *difference* we yearn for) transforms waiting into a prop of the status quo. Captivity curtails choice drastically, straitens it, but doesn't extinguish choice, neither as act nor idea, so long as the captive resists, by any and all means possible, the conditions of captivity. If the spark of resistance burns, then freedom lives.

Like a prison running smoothly because its inmates have forgotten they're incarcerated, slavery (or a state getting away with reducing civil liberties and coercing conformity without public protest because its citizens have been dumbed-down into uncritically believing their country, right or wrong, is the best damn country in the world) works best when it instills an illusion of freedom. If freedom equals the end of constant back-breaking, spirit-sapping toil, and if only the master can grant this freedom, then the slave continues to produce his daily quota—glancing up only now and then, perhaps, for signs of the Great Day shimmering on a distant horizon. The bondsman buys with his labor what he already possesses.

Like slaves, we forget that the choice to live or die empowers us to withhold labor, to rebel, to organize, to disrupt the imaginary holding us in place. We're enmeshed in a package deal, distracted, entertained, maybe a bit frustrated occasionally, but also enthralled. Rising when the conch shell bellows, donning the clothes the master distributes, gobbling the cassava we're obliged to cultivate and eat, trudging step by step at first light to work not ending till darkness (can to cain't), choice by choice exercising freedom but freedom not understood as such because at each juncture, at each step, the package deal bullies consciousness, operates to structure existence into a lockstep sequence, canceling the possibility, the memory of the power to say no. The slave's life (like mine and yours) crowded with options of a certain low order, options that subvert, subjugate, obscure options of another, primal order. We can choose blue, green, white, or yellow toilet paper, but we're not asked whether we're willing to destroy the rain forest to pay for a choice of colors. Freedom usurped, compromised by a plethora of superficial choices after someone else has set in motion a plan, a network of decisions, a package deal that decides crucial matters for us.

Michael Richardson *(Refusal of the Shadow),* inspired by the thoughts of Francis Affergan, suggests that when Martinicans voted in 1946 to incorporate Martinique into metropolitan France rather than create an independent island, they doomed themselves to a morbid simulation of identity:

> "The Martinican strives for a personal identity even in the process of denying it, thus creating a divided collective personality which, in effect, wants France but not the French. This establishes an amorous relationship based on need rather than desire. The consequence is an extinction of the self rather than the creation of an autonomous sphere of existence, since the object of desire remains unrecognized by the subject. The Martinican is in effect neither French nor West Indian, but a disembodied hybrid being unsure of its roots."

Is the only choice for Martinique either/or—French or West Indian. Why remain trapped within a racialized paradigm of essentialist oppositions—black or white, European or African. Must "hybrids" be "disembodied" and "unsure." Doesn't creolization embody the certainty of uncertainty and improvise rootedness with spontaneous performance.

Martinicans' choice of Prospero over self-determination was not made willingly, nor written in stone at a particular historical juncture, any more than Africans willingly chose to dismiss their tribal identity and become slaves or slave merchants. Identity is continuous negotiation with changing material and metaphysical circumstances. The power of contemporary would-be Prosperos is not magical, nor does it pop into existence fully formed like a genie from a bottle. The power of an oppressor can be identified, analyzed, fought and overcome. Individual insubordination, imagination, and collective social organizing are the basic ingredients of this resistance. Micro to macro refusal. Our daily choices either support or erode the material conditions condemning us into the half-asleep, half-awake vulnerability of victims.

11 JANUARY 2001

Fort-de-France—the old capital Fort-Royal renamed Fort-de-France by Napoleon, the same hero who saved the Republic by naming himself Emperor, and to please his Martinique-born Empress, Joséphine de Beauharnais, reinstated slavery on the island after it had been abolished in 1794 by the Revolutionary Council in Paris.

6:07 A.M. The shuttle bus to the plane will be leaving soon—this precise notation of time reminds me there aren't many others like it in my journal—a form of resistance or maybe I'm counting down these last sweet minutes because I'm sorry the trip's almost over—because I'm trying to prolong them—because I'm preparing myself to reenter a world where the minutes and hours of clock time rule.

We spent the last night at Hotel Caraibes—to see Fort-de-France up close and to be closer to the airport this final morning—a narrow, high bed in our room—Katrine afraid of falling out of it—thinks the height induced a panic attack awakening her in the middle of the night—panic and severe claustrophobia disturbing her sleep—some of the unpleasantness quelled by turning on the air conditioning, its drone a kind of white noise subduing sounds outside and inside.

She's still trying to catch up on missed sleep as I creep out of the room alone for coffee and last dibs on the island—find a nearby café with an outdoor sitting area—watching the world go by—notice a small, gray-bearded, buzz-cut blond guy at one of the café's outdoor tables—deeply sunken, red-rimmed eyes, the cooled-out vacancy of too many fires, too hot to handle—silver stud in one ear, whitish T-shirt and once-black, road-mangled jeans—gum-soled deck shoes—small blue backpack on one of the chairs at the table he occupies alone—he raises a cigarette to his lips—nibbles more than smokes it—van Gogh at Arles lookalike, hump of his wide-brimmed straw hat on the table—he slouches, legs stretched straight under the table, red neck exposed, leathery as the braided leather strands of the necklace around it—the end of a black leather belt, too long by many notches, droops along his thigh—torn belt loops droop too.

Another man, skinny, coal-dark, about the same uncertain middle age as the guy at the table, coming down the street on tippytoe it seems—erratic, side-to-side, slow amble, anything but one step straight after the other—almost as if he's scanning as much sidewalk as possible through the soles of his sneakers—obviously down down down on his luck—outside this early because he hadn't scrounged up any place to be inside last night—the sun up early, too, already bright and staring vacantly behind him, silhouetting the narrow ridge of his shaved head, oversize denim shorts, stick legs, coat-hanger shoulders—a dangling yellow Los Angeles Lakers T-shirt—heads toward van Gogh/Gauguin to bum a smoke—who obliges—draws a pouch of Samson tobacco, a packet of papers from a zippered compartment of backpack—taps a careful measure of tobacco onto hammock of paper—without looking up hands the embryo cigarette to the skinny guy hovering beside him—who rolls the smoke tighter, licks it shut—needs a light now—cops one when a green disposable Bic sitting beside the other man's coffee cup is raised, the big flame ignited—the dark man bends closer, cupping flame, smoke in his hands.

All this in front of the Library Schoelcher, in a kind of square or plaza opening onto that monument to eclectic excess. Good architectural intentions, I'm sure, wound up producing a bizarre structure—part pagoda, part Greek temple, part conservatory, part Gothic church, part Taj Mahal, shiny gold leaf and gold-leaf-burnished black everywhere—Corinthian column facade decorated with emblems and motifs from motley traditions. Roman arches, glassed dome, baroque, rococo ornamentation, windows of all shapes and sizes, lacy, wrought-iron balconies, a *métissage* of cathedral and shrine dedicated to Victor Schoelcher—French abolitionist, parliamentarian, republican, patriot, defender of human rights, scholar, publicist, antiquarian, collector—Martinique's Abe Lincoln, Great Emancipator of slaves. What might he have thought about the exchange we've witnessed in the almost deserted morning streets of Fort-de-France.

CHAPTER TWO

Père Labat

Père Labat becalmed in the city of La Rochelle, France. Six weeks till a ship departs for Martinique, so he waits and watches the eyes of creatures entering the tavern's darkness from the darkness beyond this black hole's thick wooden door, clumsy and stupid on its hinges as the tongue in a stutterer's mouth. Labat watching fearful eyes, suspicious eyes, bleary eyes, eyes blinking, eyes popped in owly stares, the basilisk disdain in one pair of eyes, another pair peeking out from their hiding place and gone just as quickly back to wherever they cower away their days, a sleepwalker's vacant gaze, a dreamer's eyes surprised to discover this crowd awake, raucous and busy, eyes coldly measuring, counting, calculating, eyes expressionless as a hangman's or the hangman's hooded victim, Labat a student of eyes, men's eyes a window making him privy to their souls, men's eyes foul privies of their souls. Père Labat observes and catalogues eyes till he tires of the game, tires of raising his eyes from his tankard each time the heavy door groans then scrapes through the track its metal-shod bottom edge has gouged in the tavern's stone threshold, a growling, nerve-grating alert like three-headed Cerberus barking at each patron passing through hell's portal.

Labat nods off, and the game he's been playing fades to a day at sea—not the mad, storm-tossed, treacherous sea he's been warned awaits him and the ship bound for Martinique, no—he dreams a day yet to come when the sea and sky a giant, placid eye and he searches it a whole day from the foredeck for some sign the wind might start up again, stir the mirror upon whose surface his ship is a frozen image, a ship gazing down through flat, stilled waves at drooping sails shrouding its double on the seafloor, the ghost ship sunken and drowned it must become unless a breeze snatches it from these fatal doldrums, frees it like a soul saved from the body's corruption, winged, standing to the New World.

Labat drifts, dreams, snores. Why, one Labat asks another Labat, why do men rush in here out of the night as if something or someone pursues them, why do they peer anxiously into corners as if an enemy might be concealed in the shadows, as if anyone cares about their comings and goings, as if winding up here a surprise, as if they're only pausing in this dungheap and won't stay long or may not stay at all because they have urgent business elsewhere, as if their miserable lives lead anywhere but here, waiting to scratch an "X" on a contract they can't read, waiting to be robbed or beaten or murdered or pressed into the King's service or panyared into a blackbird's doomed crew, waiting to stagger aboard the next galley to China or Peru or Guinea or the Antilles, the beguiling, blue Caribbean where his Dominican brethren have pitched a mission and plantation worked by lazy Africans, supervised by lazier priests, where Indians die like flies and the blacks die almost as fast and the colonists scheme and debauch and whine and starve and die shortly, too.

Your brethren write and pray for your assistance, for your strong arm and fertile brain and iron will, one Labat toys with the vanity of another, and a third Labat cackles at both, a parliament of Labats who, if viewed by a tavern patron, would appear to be a single monk robed in white, the visible Labat who mutters and sputters and snores, a thin line of spittle silvering his beard, sleeping in a La Rochelle tavern while his brethren beseech him, calling in the Father's name, Son's name, Saints' names or in the name of the nameless Spiritus Sanctus or in the name of Mary, Holy Mother of the Father, always begging, entreating in some name or another, the names alibis for their pride, their reluctance to admit failure or honor obligations or accept responsibility, alibis for the unnameable emptiness of their solitary lives, alibis a permanent elsewhere like those green islands marinating in turquoise waters, Carib islands stabbed by flags, by crosses, fertilized by his brethren's rotting flesh seeping from porous coffins, the wine-besotted, whore-wormed meat of the best of them mixed into island soil, and the worst, the stiff-necked, righteous, monstrous hypocrites protected by a peculiar immunity they seem to carry from birth, proof against all poisons, plagues, and disease, the brethren whose rolls of fat and simpering piety are impregnable fortresses no tropic fever can breach, survivors granted long lives to spin more mischief, bleating like sheep, bleeding like martyred virgins on the white sheet of the New World, they summon me: Come fight the Lord's good fight, Labat—lift evil's siege, cleanse the devil's shadow from these islands where we toil and struggle to spread God's word, join us on the battlefield, lend your strong arm, strong back, your stubborn will to our efforts in His name, Amen.

The sheer madness of it all offends Labat, the fecklessness and ignorance of his brethren appalls. They know nothing of Martinique, of the blacks, of the rudiments of sowing, cultivation, reaping, erecting shelter, managing men and machines. To what end this pious stretching out and laying on of hands across oceans if not to profit Church and Crown. Europe's stinking, ringed finger, fresh from its own rotting arse, extended for the New World to kiss, giggles a Labat. Hurry, hurry, embark and save the heathen whilst pagan France festers in its own putrid juices, alleys lined with starving beggars, pus oozing from their wounds, Milords, Miladies descending at night from moated towers, prowling these self-same alleys to probe, to taste the running sores. Europe a mad woman covered with scabs howling through the bars of her cage.

From this charnel house the saviors launch themselves—speckled, flaking leper's flesh hidden under brown or black or white habits, voyaging to paradise they say, seeking islands where the blood is not yet spoiled they say, to rescue the heathen they say, to wash their feet with our filthy hands, to baptize them with wine pissed from our bloated bellies.

In his dream, so close he hears the rustle of feathers, a flock of crows in billowing white skirts settles on a green field, strutting, cooing, squawking, pecking and shitting, reapers, gleaners, scavengers, cannibals.

In his small way, in his small domain Labat would insist on justice. Small justice. Precise quid pro quo balancings of reward and punishment meted out for performing work or causing harm on the plantations under his governance. Swift, implacable justice, his best reckoning, evenhanded though severe. No second guessing, no second chances. His will be done. Beyond the small matters he could dispose of as regulator of a mission's moral and commercial economy, simple decisions ensuring profitable survival of the enterprise entrusted to his hands, Labat could form no larger, abstract idea of justice in this fallen world—until, traveling as a spy in the Low Countries, he'd come upon a bizarre altarpiece, busy imps midwifing, then fattening, and finally, in the last panel of the painted triptych, torturing and slaughtering the bodies of sinners. Imps as pigs dressed in nun's habits or friar's robes gratifying herds of naked humans with a carnival of sensuous delights, imps as devils dumping bodies into the maw of a hawk-faced monster on a throne who eats then shits the revelers, converting them into piles of steaming gore. Justice the day when lowly chickens grown into giants inherit the Earth and scamper through Europe's festering cities wringing men's necks, skewering men and turning their plucked, shrieking bodies on a spit over a slow fire.

Huddled in his corner, farting to cut the stench of the others who burp and belch and soil themselves, Labat opens his eyes, would daydream more pleasantly if he could, the headman's ax, for instance, freeing mind from body with one clean stroke so each could go its merry way unencumbered by the other's complaints, Père Labat awakening to find he's not sure he's been asleep, not sure he's awake but certain he's staggered or crawled or slithered through this fugue before, that his dreams are his future and waiting drives him inward to behold it, drives him to the next task, next sea, next island where he's already landed before, playing out the fate his dreams enact, dreams he remembers, dreams he forgets until he's skulking down their dark, cobbled streets again.

Rising, nearly sick, nearly swooning when he's upright and gulps too much smoke and sour air, Père Labat steadies himself with a last eructation. Swelled to ten times his ordinary bulk, he watches the pathetic waddle and wheeze of himself through a throng of bodies to the door. Your fat arse won't squeeze through the needle's eye, another Labat hisses.

Governor Labat, your worship, Sir. For the fourth time in as many months, Sir, this one has attempted to flee. A very difficult case, your worship.

Difficult. I think not. By your barbaric singeing and plucking and lopping off you've rendered the wretch unfit for labor and, uh, propagation as well, by the gelded look of it. Do you bring this sorry creature before me to display your handiwork, your astute management of our Lord's property and estate. The case is quite simple. A ruined thing we can neither repair nor use. And since I'm not a jailer or necromancer or executioner, the resolution concerns me not. Away with it! Return the whelp to his black sire.

But stay a moment. Let it approach as near as its chain permits. Though it comprehends not a word, I wish to whisper in its remaining ear.

We are of different kinds and naturally we believe we are the better kind. We possess an all-seeing god and a sacred book assuring us we are correct in our estimation of our superiority. Just as we are born favorites of God and blessed to serve him, you are born to be our servants. From among all his creatures God has chosen us to reign, granting not only domain here on Earth but planting within our breasts an immortal soul He will gather and hold close to His bosom forever. He has sent us here to this island far from hearth and home to extend His kingdom. God offers you the inestimable bounty of his loving embrace. But you are different, the devil's spoiled children. A different kind and order. Not man, not beast, rather some vexing, dangerous, unnatural blend of both. And though we labor mightily, the soil of your hearts is stony and intractable. You refuse God's blessing. Refuse to obey. Serve the Devil, who for sport painted your skin black as his. You dishonor God's gift to you, and thus bring down His wrath upon your heads.

If you could speak a human tongue I for one would be quite curious to hear your tales. The tale of a beast-man without a soul. I have studied your savage practices, and have discovered no sense nor logic animating them, only more grotesqueries like your nakedness and sorcery, the heathen worship, excluding you from the company of godly men. Why don't you eat parrots. They are bountiful and easy to trap. Of course one must expend a bit of time and imagination in the rendering of the bird's flesh. *They all live upon fruits and seeds and their flesh contracts the odor and color of that particular fruit or seed they feed upon. They become exceedingly fat in the season when the guavas are ripe; and when they eat the seeds of the* bois d'inde *they have the odor of nutmeg and cloves, which is delightful. To prepare them for table it's best to skin them alive* (de les écorcher tout en vie) *or pluck them alive, then to make them swallow vinegar, and then to strangle them while they have the vinegar still in their throats by twisting their necks.* Some patience and ingenuity are required to learn the management of their flesh, but once mastered the particular techniques I've discovered are nearly foolproof for bringing out delicate flavors. In all modesty I've concocted more than a few savory recipes, dishes universally commended when I've shared them with guests. But you and your kind ignore parrots. You are of a different, debased order. You consume filth and abomination. Offal from the forest floor, insects, rats. You choose to live as soulless beasts so I send you back to hell as I would a beast.

Flay this bird. Then tie it to a stake. Roast it. Display it as an example to others. Hang the empty skin on a rack facing the stake and burn it, too, as you burn the creature. Let it, let them watch the infernal blackness of its pelt shrivel to ash.

When I prepare the colorful birds for the table, their squawking's almost human. Their cries and shrieks would inspire pity if I believed they suffer as men suffer. This similitude is one more of the devil's tricks. To confuse. Confound. Frustrate our mission. If we are to succeed here, if God's feast is to be served to those few able to recognize and love his power, we must deafen our ears, harden our hearts to pests we cannot convert, only exterminate. Off with this one. Let its cries ring out like sweet bells summoning the faithful to worship.

Labat recalls buying his first pair of Nikes. A stout, coconut-brown salesperson genuflects before him, the oiled crown of his head bald above a close-cropped ring of hair, an island lilt unmistakable in his nonstop, burbling pitch, bowing to tighten the boots' laces. Gathering up his white habit's skirt, now Labat can see as well as feel the elegant new footwear as he walks down a rubber runner to the front of the store and back, down and back, cushioned by magic pockets of air in the shoes' thick soles. Already tall, he strides taller by inches on layers of foam and air, a bounce in his step. It's like marching across those virgin, island beaches, the sand firm yet pliant, the New World's flesh yielding under his feet.

The clerk bustles off to attend another customer while Labat sits to consider the sneakers' extravagant price, calculating other advantages and disadvantages of purchasing them. He gazes through the scrim of New World chaos—African drums thumping from giant speakers suspended from the dome's rafters, brown, black and mongrel faces everywhere, behind counters, walking the aisles loaded down with packages, pregnant mothers pushing new babies in carts, a brace of dark, sweaty, agile, half-naked giants engaged in some sort of intense competition gliding across a screen large as a galleon's mast, gangs of whorish girls, of strutting peacock boys, thick ones, fat ones, females all butt and belly, surly, solitary rogue males, ebony faces printed on huge posters and banners glaring down from the wall with barely disguised threat and contempt, the pleased-with-themselves young adults, many exquisitely shaped and tautly muscled, bright clothes modeling their limbs and torsos like a second painted skin or draped by garments large enough for two, white ones promenading like arrogant blacks, black ones slinking like whites pale and insubstantial as ghosts through the crowd. Labat stares past the momentary discomfort of too much proximity that could be intimidating or intoxicating, even humiliating if he didn't know better, if he wasn't certain of his place, Père Labat at the mall's dead center being served, his prerogatives and privileges intact, in his hands the power still to wipe smiles off these presumptuous faces, to send them all to hell—the white, the black, the annoyingly indeterminate.

Just beyond the entrance to this island emporium, this netherworld set aside for Africanized buying and selling, dreaming and dancing, lies the sea, the roiling, tempestuous, fickle sea's roads and canyons, abysses and avalanches, its icebergs and mountainous waves taller than the tallest buildings in these skimpy New World cities, the unruly, omnipotent sea crisscrossed and disciplined, sanctified in his name, under his protection, by lanes of commerce, by treaties, cartels, syndicates, by opulent ports and sunken graveyards, by the trade winds' sweep and moan, the sea of warfare and alliance, the sea a funnel emptying black bodies onto island beaches, sucking all heaven's bounties into the coffers and palaces of Europe, the tamed, trafficked sea that brings Labat where he chooses—here, for instance, to shop—and whisks him away again, God's messenger in winged shoes like Mercury, forwarding God's plan, God's word sturdy, predictable as the truth of tide and season and prevailing wind and solid ships and the church's infallible doctrines, His word reliable as armament and instruments of navigation, the truth beyond this ridiculous moment of carnival getting and spending Labat tolerates, submits to a minute before he decides to purchase three pairs of Nikes for the long tenure he expects to endure on Martinique.

CHAPTER THREE

Fanon

Tomorrow, we must immediately take the war to the enemy,
leave him no rest, harass him, cut off his breath.
—FRANTZ FANON

Chantal

They should not be here. She's known it all along in the deep place where things you don't want to know are known. Where the knowledge of things that can hurt you or kill you, and probably will or should if they don't, never sleeps. He knew, too. They'd stayed in the newspaper office too long, too late. Night now and their color wrong here, all wrong and stupid and begging for trouble in this ghetto barrio slum estimat medina favela. She'd learned many words for it and none of them would help her now. Just before he'd hissed under his breath, *"Merde ... plus vite ... marche, Chantal ... marche plus vite ..."* She'd caught panic in

Antoine's eyes. A hopeless split-second of it naked, pleading when he thought she couldn't see his face. The big man who'd brought her here. The smart, babyish, clumsy man whose company she enjoyed because nothing seemed to surprise him. Always an order he could bark or a joke to crack. Antoine who believed he owned the world and could carry his big ideas, big money, his appetites, arrogance, and contempt anywhere he pleased.

And then … Paul asks.

She's suddenly afraid she's said too much. She was telling Paul the story to free them. Trusting him. Trusting their love. Paul and Chantal. Chantal and Paul.

Then … what happened then …

Well, nothing happened, really. We were lucky. I'm positive a man followed us. Footsteps behind us, clack, clack, clack. Neither of us dared turn around. One glimpse out of the corner of my eye enough. Could have been a shadow, could have been nothing, but it was enough. We were in a place we shouldn't be and I knew he'd found us. We belonged to him.

Stupid, yes. Very, very stupid. Night or day.

If we hadn't heard him, he'd be there anyway. You sense it in your bones. Forget about political convictions. Forget empathy. If you're white, you're scared. His feet clack-clacking the pavement almost in synch with ours, but just a little off, a little before or after. Peekaboo. Playing with our heads. Like one of those smooth, smiling guys in a club coming up for a dance and he's so good he moves half a half step off the beat, teaching you it's his music and he's in charge.

Bet you weren't thinking about dancing in the dark, sweetheart.

No. Definitely not. Dancing the last thing on my mind. I was scared. And furious because I knew the man following us wouldn't let me speak. Furious because I'd have nothing to say to his knife or gun except, Why. Please don't hurt me.

Paul

On the screen they are chopping up Patrice Lumumba and burning his body parts in an oil drum. Two thick, red-faced, unhappy louts. Bruegel peasants sweating through khaki uniforms, working overtime to clean up the King's mess. I imagine Chantal beside me, imagine us going to a bar after the movie, and maybe I'd attempt to explain my reaction when I was a kid and first heard Lumumba's name. His name and the others—Kasavubu, Mobutu, Tshombe. Names embarrassing me, sounding like tom-toms, like jibber-jabber blabbered through big African lips at Tarzan or Bwana in Hollywood movies. Black, sweaty faces. Fat eyes rolling and showing too much white. Would I tell her I'd heard my white friends giggling inside my skull at the funny names even as the news reported rape, massacres, chaos in faraway countries. Terrified Europeans fleeing, wild Africans seizing power. Mumbo jumbo names. Cannibal names. Nigger names coming to get me. Lumumba-Tshombe-Mobutu-Kasavubu.

O my body,
make of me a man who always asks questions!
—FRANTZ FANON

Paul

In Accra, Ghana, in 1960, Frantz Fanon met Patrice Lumumba. Both spoke French, both were 34, and in the next year both would die. Lumumba murdered in the Congo at the beginning of 1961, Fanon succumbing to leukemia in Washington, D.C., at year's end.

Today I'm much older than these dead men lived to be, these fallen heroes once old enough to be my fathers. How could this be. Everything and nothing changing. When Lumumba and Fanon died, I was a boy setting out to conquer a world that, by disposing of them, had already unequivocally expressed its scorn, its determination to prevent boys like me from conquering much of anything. Mercifully or unmercifully I knew next to nothing about either man back in 1961. Full of myself, studying hard to win a college scholarship, I was intoxicated by what I believed were infinite possibilities, unlimited time. The lives and deaths of Fanon and Lumumba, the places where they'd been born mostly blank regions on the map of my imagination, dark and negative if not blank, irrelevant to the hazy plans I daydreamed for my future. Now I understand (and believe me, derive no satisfaction from the fact) that my ignorance of these men, their countries, their legacy, did not indicate simply a personal failure of imagination. Particular kinds of information and knowledge had been erased by my education. Erased ruthlessly, systematically, with malice, just as Patrice Lumumba, Frantz Fanon, and countless others—perhaps our best women and men—have been struck down and erased.

I've long been able to tell how long a guerrilla has been fighting by the look in his eyes. Eyes like this do not lie. They say quite openly that they have seen terrible things: repression, torture, shellings, pursuits, liquidations ... You see a sort of haughtiness in such eyes, and an almost murderous hardness. And intimidation. You quickly get into the habit of being careful in dealing with men like these. You can tell them everything, but they have to be able to feel and touch the revolution in the words you use. Very difficult to deceive, to get around or infiltrate—

—FRANTZ FANON

Paul

We did not recognize the face stenciled with black spray paint on a greenish-gray metal shed (whose purpose we did not recognize either) in a field that Chantal and I passed by each day on our walks to the beach. Though we remained slightly curious about this somehow familiar face staring back at us in the middle of nowhere, curious about the partly effaced writing beneath it—Arabic script, I guessed, so the words incomprehensible to us even if intact—the face a small detail during the two weeks we spent in Martinique over a Christmas holiday, enjoying tropical sea and sun, gorging ourselves on the sudden, unexpected bounty of a powerful mutual attraction transforming itself into something richer, deeper. Busy fucking our brains out, so to speak. In doggy heat, dazed, falling in love. Martinique a perfect third partner, multiplying the permutations and combinations of pleasing each other, an erotic presence nibbling, coddling, provoking, goading, overloading our senses, enslaving us subtly as we became accustomed to the constant attention of sun, palm trees sighing, the surf's murmur, the breeze's caressing fingers. And once it had registered, the face, like the island's beguiling complicity, never entirely disappeared.

Strangely, we seemed to be the only ones who saw it. Not only couldn't the hotel staff, other guests, or local shopkeepers name the face, they claimed to be unaware of its existence in the field where a few pale, long-horned cattle were tethered near the road's edge to graze. Could the face be there and not there. One of the island's fabled ghosts playing us. If we stopped looking, if we blinked, would it go away.

One afternoon a young man on a bicycle, his small, round head bristling with spiky braids, pedaled idly toward us, zigzagging from one edge of the road to the other, and reached us just as we were opposite the shed. In English, French, and sign language we hailed him. He stopped his undersize bike, straddled it, supporting its weight with one foot on the ground. When we asked about the face, he stared hard, as if surprised a structure had sprouted in the field since his last trip up the road, then firmly shook his head no, no, turning over his hands to prove how they, too, were innocent.

Clearly he wished to be helpful, but he looked once more at the shed and shrugged his bare, bony shoulders. Then the boy's turn to be curious, glancing at Chantal, meeting my gaze for the first time before hiding his eyes behind long, curled lashes. I could hear his thoughts. Whoever else I'd become, wouldn't I always be a shy, skinny brown kid on a bike. Who are these strangers worried about a face painted on the side of a metal box, a beat-up face and gang tags and scribble-scrabble writing. Why are these people minding my business, stopping me, bothering me about a face nobody sees, this man dark as me and this blond woman with nothing better to do than stroll, white hand in black hand, half-naked, like trouble itself up and down my road, on my island asking questions about stuff nobody cares about, not asking my name, not offering some little work and tip? Why else they think I be pedaling the livelong day up and back, up and back scuffling for a little change.

When Chantal and I reached the entrance to the beach, I checked back over my shoulder. The boy hadn't moved from the spot where we'd left him, the miniature bike, his long, lean body side-saddle astride it printed hazily against the glare, a Giacometti stick figure frozen yet moving. Staring into an empty field.

Fanon didn't claim the crude, spray-painted replica of his face until I recalled he'd been born there, on the French island of Martinique. Once that connection had reconnected in my brain, other memories were freed—his face in a photo snapped during the first *Présence Africaine* conference in Paris in the 1950s, his face on the back cover of *The Wretched of the Earth,* a color shot of him illustrating a magazine review of *Black Skin, White Masks.* Of course it's Frantz Fanon. Who else. Why had it taken me so long to recognize him. Was I gradually, or maybe not so gradually, forgetting everything I'd learned, the pace quickening the more I read. Losing what's come before, as more stuff, instantly lost, disappears before it even has a chance to sink in, stir up the mix and be properly remembered or forgotten.

On the rooftop of my apartment building, the draft of the Fanon book open, waiting for me to begin again, I had been recalling that time on Martinique with Chantal when we splurged the advance on my first novel and Fanon's face had intruded. Then I noticed an enormous plume of dark smoke billowing above the skyline. A continuous scream and hoot and whine of sirens began echoing from the streets below. Before long, tenants who'd been watching TV began to gather on the roof. From their stunned, disbelieving comments I learned planes had rammed the Twin Towers. The giant buildings burning.

A few days before, in an oddly begrudging, ambivalent biography of Frantz Fanon authored by a guy who seemed basically to despise, mistrust, underestimate Fanon's intelligence even as he painstakingly constructed a monumental life for his subject, I had read that Fanon defined the *Third World* as a *colossal mass* facing Europe and that the Third World's *project* must be to resolve problems to which Europe has found no solutions. Now a churning black cloud of smoke, skyscrapers on fire. Somebody had gotten tired of waiting. Somebody had launched their version of problem-solving.

In this becalmed zone the sea has a smooth surface, the palm tree stirs gently in the breeze, the waves lap against the pebbles, and raw materials are ceaselessly transported, justifying the presence of the settler: and all the while the native, bent double, more dead than alive, exists interminably in an unchanging dream.

—Frantz Fanon

Paul

According to the dreadlocked brother waiting tables at Aunt Kizzy's snack stand, this road we're on should take us to

Martinique's best beaches. I'm losing faith as the road narrows, roughens, ain't hardly road no more, an obstacle course of steep ruts, hulking boulders, potholes, a mud-colored track between margins definitely not road, to my left reedy muck that probably could swallow the rental car without a burp, to my right squatty trees whose gray roots and branches braid into an impenetrable tangle running low along the ground. Glimpses of ocean remind me why I'm dodging rocks, dropping blindly over precipices where there might or might not be more road for the tires to grab.

After a short climb paralleling a rocky wall that blocks our view, we reach a flat crest and below us, a mile down a sloping shelf of stone, the sea sparkles, visible to the horizon. I slow the car to take in the view. Erosion has pocked and furrowed the immense stone's steep flanks with cracks, crevices, caves, and just beyond a jumble of huge, flat rocks edging the stone formation, yes, yes, golden sand stretches. A few bodies are visible sunning on exposed ledges or hunkered in shaded recesses of the stony cliff, but the beach appears empty as paradise.

Smoother now, the road descends as abruptly as it rose, continues on level ground. Woods conceal the water until we reach a line of tall trees canopied by a web of interlaced branches and leaves. Through black trunks, straight and bare as poles, we can see crackling ocean, sand bleached nearly white just before it meets turquoise water.

This is what we've been looking for. Hungry for. Remember how quickly we unpacked the car. You never looked more gorgeous, girl. Your orange sarong transparent as orange tissue paper as you weave between trees, step over their sprawling roots, *chaloupe* in and out of shafts of light spilling through the green roof. Even now, with the power to invent a dream-perfect day, I'd change nothing about the blue sky, hot sun, white-capped breakers churning on miles of gloriously vacant beach. Wouldn't alter a single detail of the laughing, shiny woman striding through the shadowy anteroom, muscling more than her share of stuff we figured we'd require so we wouldn't have to stir for the rest of the day once we'd selected a spot and plopped down on the sand.

Just beyond the wooded margin of beach, scattered here and there in a widely spaced line paralleling the shore, a different variety of tree with long, gnarly octopus arms and leaves like green ping-pong paddles. We choose one that will provide protection against the evil midday rays of the sun. Behind it a cool black sanctuary to stash our bottled water, in front low branches to dry wet towels and swimsuits. A thick, triple-barreled trunk secludes us from cars passing on the road or anybody approaching on foot. Room for both of us to rest our backs against the tree, in sun or shade depending on how you angle yourself. Front-row seats with an unimpeded view of sea and sky.

We swim naked. Or rather you swim and I play in water up to my chest, performing my clumsy riff on body surfing, wishing I'd learned to be a fish like you. When you pop out of the water next to me, grinning from ear to ear, hair plastered snaky to your skull, bright beads of water sticking to your lashes and pearled in your ears, you look so fine I have to scoop you up in my arms. Breakers smack our backs, splash our faces. We can't hear each other over the water's roar, shouting and laughing anyway at whatever silliness we holler back and forth. I walk out deeper, a step too deep and a wave punches my feet out from under me and we're suddenly submerged, then bob like corks, the current in charge, spinning, dragging, tossing our bodies. I lose my grip on you and you stroke away, dive into a foaming wall of water, while I flounder, spitting, coughing, trying to catch my breath. Arms flailing like I'm beating out a fire.

Near a tree like ours a couple with enormous backpacks and two young kids appear. Damn, we're both thinking, here comes suburbia, here come rules saying we have to put on clothes. But in the time it takes you to pull your orange sarong out of the wicker basket and drape it over your legs and me to retrieve damp gym shorts from a branch, the newcomers have abandoned homemaking. Bare-assed as seals, they dash into the sea.

During the afternoon more company arrives. Strollers up and down the beach. Some clothed, some not. So it's demi-paradise, roll your own rules. The beach less and more private. Less because other people around. More because we can choose to ignore them.

A new pleasure—your naked body in bright sunlight. New colors, new textures. You with your back resting against a towel against the rough bark of the platypus-pawed tree, reading your book, and me sprawled on my belly, sometimes reading, but I couldn't keep my eyes off you, your body's simple ease, your bare legs steepled and spread, painted toes digging in the sand.

You allowing me to see you in ways I never have before, inviting me inside, past the mysterious gates of the body no one can enter without permission, no matter how hard they stare at our skin, its colors, textures, patches of hair.

No need to cover up, you decide. Nothing to hide from strangers meandering along the water's edge, nor a European guy tanned parchment as a native who settles down nearer, maybe thirty yards away, spreading out his towel nonchalantly, pretending to ignore us but really—I spy on him as intently as he spies on you—can't take his eyes off you, but that's okay too, you decide, no need to conceal what he can't see. Were you teasing him when you slid your hips in his direction, letting him know you're the boss, you can turn his gaze away, even if his eyes were as close to you as mine.

I thought I might have slain my demons that day watching another man's eyes on you, a white guy no less. I believed I was free of jealousy that day and maybe in the days to come if I stayed lucky, stayed clear about what belonged to you, belonged to me, what could or couldn't be stolen from us, what couldn't be owned or possessed.

At whatever level we study it—relationships between individuals, new names for sports clubs, the human admixture at cocktail parties, in the police, on the directing boards of national or private banks—decolonialization is quite simply the replacing of a certain "species" of men by another "species" of men.

—FRANTZ FANON

Paul

Last night my head was spinning. Stumbling out of bed to piss, I cursed myself, cursed the inventor of wine. No need to check the clock. Every night *3 A.M.* crouches in the dark, waiting to jump me, tortures confessions from me for a couple of hours till I'm too exhausted to go back to sleep. Then it's nearly dawn, every nerve cell in my body buzzing, whining. I start to dread the coming day, the slow drag through it with all my energy drained before the day starts. And when the day ends, I'll be too tired to fall asleep. Even if I drift off some nights from sheer exhaustion, in a minute a voice whispers in my ear, "Hey, it's me, *3 A.M.,* your friendly terrorist, here to inform you it's time."

No, I'm not writing you to complain, Chantal. I'm surviving unhappiness. In fact, apart from my sleep being mugged every night, I'm doing reasonably okay. Better than I should be with so much misery and murder banking up higher and higher just outside my door. Why should anybody sleep soundly these days. The clock's ticking. Time's running out. The *haves* lie down each night in a house full of servants plotting their doom. The *have-nots* flop down, if they have a place to flop, knowing the same shitty ole lives will greet them in the morning. So maybe nobody's sleeping well. Shouldn't be if we are. My 3 A.M. blues a reminder I'm not exempt. I can't be black and white, rich and poor, guilty and innocent. Know what I mean, jellybean. Ashes, ashes, we all fall down.

So I guess I'm writing to fuss about the state of the world and to say hello to you. How are you today, my sweet one. And where, oh where. Do you ever think about our island. Since I've lost touch with you, I can't mail this epistle, but I promise to bundle myself up in it and walk the streets like one of those sandwich-board people wearing the words for everybody to read. Perhaps a kind stranger will get the message and pass it on to another stranger and so forth till one day a stranger passes it on to you. Wouldn't that be something. Would it delight and impress you enough to bring me back from the dead? You back from the dead? Where, oh where has my sweet lamb strayed.

When my restless hands caress these white breasts, they grasp white civilization and dignity and make them mine.

—Frantz Fanon

New York

From the stories you tell me, you were conducting a one-woman campaign to improve France's relationship with its territories *outre-mer.* Mali, Guadeloupe, Algeria, Martinique, Ivory Coast, Senegal. What about Madagascar, France really fucked with Madagascar. Any boyfriends from over there.

Chantal smiles. You must understand what it was like in Paris. Strikes in the universities. Workers and students rallying side by side in the streets. Every day a circus. We wanted change. Wanted the whole world to change. We were very happy to offer our bodies, our lives to bring about change. In a New World we wouldn't need diplomas, wouldn't need our parents' bourgeois possessions and values. Women began to speak out. Step out of men's shadows, our mother's shadows. Why not do as we please. Why not ten lovers or a hundred lovers. We claimed our sexuality. Enjoyed it, gloried in it. Hadn't men always been smart enough to take what they desired. Weren't women equally smart—equally free—strong.

Sounds like fun. Wish I'd been around for the party. But

what you're saying still doesn't explain how come you kept winding up in black men's arms.

Not only black men but more than white. That's true, yes. I was attracted more by black men. To my eyes they … you … are more beautiful. More fun.

Forbidden fun.

Yes and no. Not like in America. But if you went with a black man, even in those wild times, you were testing white French people. I admit I liked pushing past the edge a bit. I've always chosen men, white ones, black ones, who were outsiders. My first serious lover an Algerian. A beautiful man. Very smart. I didn't choose him simply because he was darker. I was attracted by his politics. The way he was French and not French. In the cafés he and his friends constantly talked politics, but more than the café talk, it was the stories he told me about his family, how they suffered after they emigrated to France. To grow, I needed to hear those stories.

Kamal didn't preach to me. I'd had enough preaching from professors at school, my father at home. I was running from people telling me how to live my life. Angry at myself for obeying too long. From Kamal I learned things about my country, myself, I'd never dreamed. I became ashamed of France. So much hate. So deep and ugly. An education preparing me for your country, Paul.

Worse here.

Maybe. Certainly not better.

Worse.

The struggle no longer concerns the place where you are but the places where you are going. Each fighter carries his warring country between his toes.
—Frantz Fanon

Chantal

She calls out his name: Antoine. He doesn't answer, and she undresses quiet as a thief. Welcomes for once Antoine's loud snoring. Adjusts her movements in the dark room to the metronome of wheezes and snorts, his labored breathing another kind of darkness into which she can slip from shadow to shadow unnoticed. Though her head said no, her heart had once whispered, take a chance, love this man, but her body, too, shook its head, no, no, huh-uh.

Stepping into the hotel room from its balcony overlooking the bay, she recalls her body's reluctance, how it continues to insist it desires more than this man would ever be able to give. This bearish man she cares for even as she tiptoes around the bed where he is snoring, hoping he won't awaken, hoping he'll drop off peacefully to sleep, a magic hibernation allowing them to enjoy days on the island together, reserving the nights for her to be alone with her body, heeding its advice, coaxing out its memories, treating herself to the company of missing others, her fingers private and relentless as she caresses herself, folding herself deeper and deeper into other nights, preferring imagined sex with other men to sex with him. Sex with him not exactly perfunctory. Not bad sex. Just sex going nowhere. Coupling because it's pleasant to snuggle and couple before sleep. Afterward, her body to deal with, the body still reluctant, still only vaguely engaged, standing off somewhere, desiring much, much more, still wagging its stubborn head *why, why.*

She wills her limbs weightless as she lifts the sheet, settles into bed beside him. Considers a moment the broad back looming next to her, the option of wrapping her arms around his warm, furry bulk. He would feign annoyance, grunt his displeasure at being awakened till she pinches a knob of flesh at his waist or brushes her palm across his tiny nipples or reaches under his belly to cup his soft, sleepy penis. Then if she's patient and he's in the mood, the Earth would roll over and cover her, pressing down dark, heavy, rubbing her flesh with its heft.

After a while, when his ponderous thrusts just weight and wiggle atop her, she'd squeeze her eyes shut and hold her breath to the edge of suffocation, letting him crush her flesh and bones, sink into her, empty her, stubborn till the blackness engulfing her flashes blue, holding her breath till her lungs and heart automatically rebel, till fear was real and she'd panic *have I waited too long, let the Earth bury me too deeply,* gasping for air, sucking air in huge, hungry gulps while she squirms beneath him to reopen the flattened cavities of her chest and belly, her hips and thighs thrashing to snatch back their share of air.

The thrashing, gasping routine played out once, once always enough to excite the shuddering spill of him inside her, his starved whimper of satisfaction or disgust or both.

Was it cheating to let him think these mini-deaths were signs of passion whipping her about.

One night she'd asked him, because he was Antoine and she could ask him anything, if he overheard his squeaky, begrudged little cry and what he thought it might mean. Stop, he said, shooing her question away with a flutter of one thick pale hand. She couldn't stop. Wondered if he, too, needed to trick her, trick himself into believing their coupling more than it was. Why would he bother. Did what she felt matter to him, after all. What mattered to Antoine or any man beyond ending the chase, the frantic last-ditch pumping that frees him from himself, frees him of desire for the woman he'd caught.

Careful not to awaken him, she grazes the hillock of his hip with her fingertip, a touch so light it may not be actual touch, just mimicked touch outlining his shape in the air, recalling their all-night conversations, how the fucking or not fucking beforehand mattered so much less than the chatter chatter chattering while smoke from his endless Gitanes circled the dark room.

The Island

You're telling it this way to keep me from being jealous.

You jealous of him. Why. Years since I've seen Antoine. Why are we talking about him.

Sorry. I just don't think you're being exactly honest with me. Or yourself. You were lovers for years. C'mon. That ain't no casual affair. Something more there you're not admitting.

No. No. No. I've known him a long time. But no way we were lovers that long. Never really lovers, you might say. Not love like we have. For years at a time I might not see him.

Except when he called, you'd go, right. And be lovers again, right.

You're not listening. I told you the sex was a small part of it. Not about that … never.

Somehow it always happened, though, didn't it. The sex. You made yourself available. Whatever the attraction, I can't stand the idea of his power over you. Was it his whiteness, maybe. A little bit of variety, a little French boy homecoming for you. Proving to yourself you could still be white, if you chose.

Stop being an idiot. If he was passing through the city and I had no attachments, why not see him. I never said I didn't enjoy his company. He's a smart man. And funny. So if I was free when he called, we'd get together. It happened a few times over the years. I never wanted more. Believe me, I could have made it more. I'm sure he liked me, but I knew better than to fall in love with a man like him. He was terrible with women.

Okay. Maybe you were smart enough not to fall in love. But you weren't willing to give up on him, either. You left the door open. Let him use you.

We used each other. He offered a trip to the Caribbean. It was winter. I was between jobs. Broke. Depressed. I was lonely, needy, and the city can be so gray and horrible in February. A week on a tropical island. Why would I say no.

More than a job, wasn't it. You both understood quite well he was offering more than a job. He bought you. Bought you like they always buy what they want.

He was my friend. A man who could make me laugh. Of course I said yes.

If a condition of the bargain is sleeping with him, isn't that more than friendship.

Is it. No one forced me to do anything. I chose to go. Enjoyed the trip. I needed to be away from the city. From my troubles. Needed a little fun. Needed a man to look after me, make me feel like a woman.

I guess he did just that, huh. Made you feel like a woman.

No. Not the way I feel with you. Not the way I feel here with you on our island, my love. Please stop. A different time, different place, then. Not our island.

Different, you say. Another island, you say. So what if it was some other goddamn island.

Chantal

She's alone, sitting up in bed watching dawn ignite the window blind's edges, arms clasped around her drawn-up knees, remembering their last morning on Martinique, how quiet Paul had become. As if his rage the night before hadn't happened. Nor the love-making after. No more questions. Was it the weight of silence blurring Paul's face, dissolving his features as he glanced around the room at nothing, anything to avoid her eyes. He's any man, no man, all of them quiet as puddles seeping into the damp soil of a green green grassy field after a thunderstorm. She remembers his unfocused stare, the last, sad smile when, finally, he got up to pack. Remembers herself naked in this same posture, his sperm dry, itchy little flakes in her pubic hair. Wonders—would Paul be jealous today if she told him she found the hurt of his beautiful smile hovering in Osama bin Laden's eyes.

We must not therefore be content with delving into the past of a people in order to find coherent elements which will counteract colonialism's attempts to falsify and harm. We must work and fight with the same rhythm as the people to construct the future and to prepare the ground.

—Frantz Fanon

Chantal

Somewhere in the crippled vastness of this city Paul sits grumbling with the Fanon book he'll never finish. Does this certainty, these facts comfort her on a gray morning when chill air mists the suddenly vulnerable windows on the top floor where she lives, the wind's moaning and groaning amplified as it swirls around jutting balconies, gusts into corners, shrieks from ground to roof in shafts formed by wings of the high-rise converging with its body. Sounds like a gigantic wet towel outside stinging the building's flanks and she expects to see bricks peeling away, toppling, falling in rows precise as geese after she wipes the glass dry with the heel of her hand, but instead needles of rain slant down, invisible unless she stares and stares.

Paul diligently poring over yellow sheets of tablet paper, cramped, scrawled words written, unwritten, rewritten, layers of words too thickly impacted for anyone not him to decode. If he can, if he'll ever bother. Hunched over a desk or slumped in a cushioned armchair. Yes. A mug of sludgy black coffee near at hand. How many mornings had she awakened to the scene. Yes. Fascinating at first. Reassuring. Like knowing the sun will rise because you can count on the ancient guy who drives the chariot. Rain or shine you know the light of Paul's apartment will burn yellow before dawn. Snapped on every morning while you sleep. Snapped on whether you wake up or not. He'll be there. Steadfast. Undistractable. His reliability more than a routine. It's his nature. What he's become, who he is. You can count on it.

But once you're sure, when you know you can expect him to be sitting, worrying a manuscript no matter what else is going on in the world, doesn't the steadiness begin to grate, lose its luster. Some mornings her resentment palpable. She'd want to hit him. Blurt out *"How dare you?"* Worse than all that, finally, was boredom. Getting used to him, almost sorry for him once she understood he had no choice.

Maybe it wasn't so bad after all to be certain of his company when she awakened, company no matter how negative, how abstract. Paul out there, wherever she found herself, rain-soaked morning or dry. Out there for sure and for sure this morning she's missing him, wants to grab him by the scruff of the neck, rattle his bones, shake him out of his dream. You're missing it, man. Missing and missed.

I can write only the present, he'd said, because the past is too complicated. I remember the past too well. The present's easy to forget. Nobody remembers the present anymore. So it's easy to forge. Easy to turn into fiction.

She recalls the notion of negative dependability from some literary pundit's discussion of narrative technique. How certain characters couldn't help themselves. They lied because they knew no other way. Lied even when the truth would obviously serve them better. Always twisting or exaggerating the facts or flat out making up shit to suit their purposes, their only purpose to lie. Do such people offer a ray of hope in an undependable world. If you precisely discounted what they said, scrupulously deflated or inflated or reversed or ignored or denied it, could you approximate truth. Reliably estimate at least what wasn't so. Is that why Paul declared his Fanon book must be fiction. Is it why she reads romances voraciously, giggling at her credibility, her sentimental naïveté while she turns pages and weeps. If she subtracts the lies she wishes to believe and adds the untruths that liars tell, could she calculate the truth of her life, the truth of this dying metropolis through whose wet, heavy air she sends Paul a greeting this morning, wishing she could sing it, wishing he'd hear her voice, jump up and dance.

New York

If I'd guessed the face on the shed would fascinate you long after you stopped needing to see mine, I would have been jealous.

Whoa. Hold on, lady. Who said I stopped needing you. Aren't you forgetting you're the one who deserted me and flew back to Paris.

Why do you say such a thing. You know I didn't simply pack up and leave. You know you left me no choice. Anyway, I came back, didn't I.

I'm still not sure why. Or why you split. Maybe you were jealous of the face. Or some goddamn face. Unhappy from the beginning. Even on Martinique when things were just about perfect. When I believed we were in love.

Of course we were in love. The proof—both of us insanely

jealous all the time. Me more jealous than you, though you were the one always talking about your jealousy. About my past. My color. I think you used them as weapons. Kept me explaining myself, defending myself so I couldn't speak of my own hurt. I left New York because I couldn't stand the images of you naked with that woman. Your hands in her hair. Touching her. Her looking at your body. Sometimes I'd want to scream. Those images took away all my confidence. My security. Nothing special about me. About us. Who was I. Just the latest in a long line of bodies. The newness would soon wear off and you'd begin looking for newness. We'd just returned from Martinique and it had already started with her. A mistake, you said. Said you were angry, confused. Never again, you promised. But why. Why wouldn't it happen again.

You shouldn't have let your anger fester. You should have talked to me.

Really. Should I have been like you. Waking me up in the middle of the night. Calling me *white bitch.* Refusing to touch me, to look at me. Demanding embarrassing details. Insisting I tell you everything when there was nothing to tell. Is that how I should have acted.

I loved you. I needed to understand you.

You did love me. Or believed you did. It doesn't matter now. After Martinique you kept pushing, pushing till you found a way out. Till I said too much or didn't say enough. And the whole time I never uttered a word about my pain. When I finally did, it was too late. Something inside me had been broken. I could only scream. Or run.

Fanon's face.

What about his face.

When we saw it, when it broke the silence, it was already too late. We'd lost our chance. He was already dead.

Oh, not the Africa of poets, the Africa that is sleeping, but the Africa that stops you sleeping because the people are impatient to be doing something, to speak and to play. The people who are saying: "We want to make ourselves a people, we want to build, love, respect and create." The people who weep when you say "I come from a country where the women have no children and children have no mothers." The people who sing "Algeria, our brother country, a country that is calling out, a country that hopes."

—FRANTZ FANON

Chantal

So there you were, huh. White woman with a white man at night in one of the most dangerous, blackest, poorest sections of one of the most dangerous black cities anywhere on Earth and you weren't thinking about dancing, right, you were scared shitless and this big-deal, big-guy buddy or boss or lover or fellow fool—whatever—he's shaking in his booties, too. What I want to know is not so much why. People usually have reasons, lame-brained or otherwise, for what they do, so I assume your reasons probably made sense to you at the time—a deadline maybe for your project and pushing to finish or maybe the work fascinating and you got caught up, lost track of the hour, or maybe you'd been on the island long enough to start feeling comfortable, everybody nice to you, showing you around, hanging out at night in the clubs with the locals, smoking ganja with the Rasta brothers in the hills, feeling you're different, loved in spite of centuries of white crimes against the people—the daily misery and humiliation of arriving at the threshold of the twenty-first century and still being starved, robbed, beaten in what's spozed to be your own goddamn country, still a boy or a wench bending over and taking it up the ass for tips tourists toss at you. Maybe you believed you'd transcended that boring old-school, colonized and colonizer, oppressed and oppressor bullshit and could start fresh, a new world order and everybody just people after all—all colors, shapes, sizes, smells, but just plain folks after all. Shit. Or maybe you and your rich white fella finished work in the office he'd rented for his project and got horny thinking about the pretty, half-naked brown men and women, the flesh surrounding you every day on the island, the island lilt of their voices, how their hips sway and shoulders dip and butts pout, their flimsy native clothes more come-on than cover-up, to say nothing of the drums, the singing and dancing, the sticky web of sunshine and sparkling sea snaring your senses, pumping them up so you turn off your cell phones, shut the books, pack away your papers and computers, lock the office door, and get it on—the whole sweaty, heavy-breathing nasty atop a desk, spiced by images of handsome natives brushing past you on the busy streets. Brown muscles, brown dicks and titties, brown funk, bushy hair. It might have been a sudden irresistible pussy call kept you late at the office, but like I said before the reason's not what really interests me. I want to know what you imagined. Who you believed you were. Two white Europeans parading after dark through the grungiest, most unforgiving, most violent quarter of the town. The two of you well-fed, tanned, pretty. *Beg pardon folks, just passing through,* through the cesspool your bad intentions and good intentions created, a sewer where human beings must make lives for themselves swimming in centuries of your filth. What did you imagine yourselves doing. What do you imagine you're doing here on this island with me. Whatever your reasons, what gives you the right to rub the privilege of your whiteness, your immunity in dying people's faces. Slinking through a place so down and out niggers with nothing to lose avoid it if they can. Dog-eat-dog back-of-the-wall and at night too. Who the fuck did you think you were. What kind of daydream were you two strolling around in.

She survived it. That's all she can say for sure. Or wishes to say to herself, reflecting on that time now. Survived the stupid, trespassing night. Survived Paul's harangue years after the night. Survived the end of their time together. Their trip to the island Paul could not keep separate from other trips, other islands, other men. Survived his dark hands on her, shaking her shoulders. His screaming. Hers.

Survived it in a fashion, she's quick to add, reminding herself or whomever she's speaking to this morning that surviving covers lots of ground, that survival may be everything and it's also nothing. Checks herself, wonders if she really means that, checks the eyes of the one she's addressing, it could be Paul, him here next to her quietly listening, his eyes filling up with tears as he follows where she leads, into the abyss, the chances they'd squandered, the scorched earth, his scorched fingers digging into her scorched flesh, wanting to hurt, to rip, shaking her till she submits, her head flopping side to side as he looms over her, shaking, shaking, shaking whiteness out and blackness in or blackness in and whiteness out, she remembers thinking some crazy true thought like that just before she stopped thinking and let her body have its way, shaken, sinking.

Today I believe in the possibility of love.
—Frantz Fanon

Revenants
They say that toward the end of her life or you could say when her life was over the cops gathered up what was left of Marilyn Monroe after she'd finally binged enough booze and pills to kill herself and rushed her body to Bellevue or some other mental ward where she was stripped and deposited in a padded, brightly lit quiet room. Throughout the night, as word of her presence spread, a steady trickle of cops and hospital personnel arrived to take turns peering through the peephole of the cubicle where Marilyn Monroe lay on display naked, sleeping her drugged last sleep.

Think of poor Marilyn Monroe, then try to visualize Frantz Fanon's final days in a Washington, D.C., hospital room, curious doctors, nurses, interns trooping in and out to observe Fanon, this Fanon they'd heard awful things about, a fiery, white-hating revolutionary, prophet of terror, now helpless, dazed, unable to speak, dying of leukemia, a disease characterized by an overload of leukocytes, white corpuscles in the blood that suppress other cells. Fanon seized by fits of vomiting and diarrhea as he fights to rid his system of poison, poison causing hyperpigmentation, his skin turning blacker and blacker, like Patrice Lumumba's skin as his body parts cooked in a rusty oil barrel. Fanon and Marilyn chained together, stuffed in the hold of a slave ship crossing the Atlantic. Naked, shitting, pissing, throwing up on each other as the creaking wooden vessel's tossed by stormy seas. Then, during a calm, they are hauled on deck to dance. What should we name the dance they perform under the eyes of the crew, the dance timed by a crackling cat-o'-nine-tails a drunken sailor snaps at their bare, filthy, bloody, beautiful backs.

Hello. My name is Marilyn.

Hi. I'm Frantz.

Haven't we met before.

It could have happened.

Hard to be sure, isn't it. It's so dark below. And so dazzling up here. I have to squint to see you. How can they keep staring at us without going blind.

Perhaps they are blind. Perhaps we are, too.

Here, take my hand.

Take my temperature, my blood pressure, my pulse.

Why are they doing this. Why can't they take their eyes off us. What do they expect to see.

I'm very sick. I arrived in this country sick and they put something in my food every day to make me sicker. I'm worried I won't survive to finish my book.

Don't worry. You'll finish. And I promise to read every word.

Maybe we won't die. Maybe there's hope. Hope for the ones not born yet.

I'm so cold. Hold me. Never let me go.

I never thought you … I never thought we would end up like this.

It doesn't end like this. This is just a dream. We're trapped in their nasty dreaming. Sleep, sleep, my pumpkin. Soon we'll wake up in another dream. Everything will be different …

Happy birthday to you,
Happy birthday to you!
Happy birthday, dear Frantz.

CHAPTER FOUR

The Island

Outside my window snow covers lawns, banks of it a couple of feet deep bury the curbs, whiteness lines branches, clings to pine needles, clots crotches where limbs join tree trunks. In May 1902, when refugees fleeing Mount Pelée's tremors began arriving, the citizens of St.-Pierre noticed that these sudden, frightened visitors (and all their possessions hastily bundled and transported with them) were dusted with a coat of fine whitish ash. *Petite neige.* Little snow. Though it had yet to reach St.-Pierre, the ash had been raining for weeks on villages to the north and east of the capital city. Then dark, ominous columns of smoke rising from Mount Pelée's summit had become visible from St.-Pierre streets, and villagers fleeing the surrounding countryside reported how the Earth shook more violently each night and they'd awaken to find a veil of whiteness draping roofs, fields, trees, the already ghostly pale cattle. *Petite neige.*

Why did island people blessedly innocent of winter's rigors call this ash presaging their doom *snow.*

It had taken us till dusk to reach the ruins and now, standing on top of a hill where once a huge church, municipal center, and clock tower had reigned, looking past the muddle of broken stones, past the black fringe of treetops poking over the hill's crest, we could see the sky and below it the ocean darkening by visible degrees as light drained rapidly from the air, and after stepping closer to the edge see St.-Pierre's harbor, then miles and miles of shoreline and mountains sloping gently down to meet it, a striking panorama that might have ravished you even on the terrible morning you paused just outside the cathedral door, in the shadow of one of the Corinthian columns supporting its mammoth portico, and gazed back over your shoulder a moment at ridge echoing rippling ridge until the mountains merge seamlessly with distant clouds, a view veiled by the strange grayish pallor of a dawn like none you'd ever witnessed before, the morning after a night when the Earth never ceased trembling and shuddering like some fever-stricken giant whose nightmare had gripped you in its fist, a tortured, merciless giant whose breath shot up in black, swaying columns from the conical mountain squatting behind you, Mount Pelée's vastness dwarfing the bulk of the church into which your family has trooped, frightened, eyes red-rimmed from crying and sleeplessness, throats parched from the rain of dry, hot cinders the angry mountain has been disgorging on St.-Pierre for a week, you lingering behind your wife and children as if your puny rearguard vigilance, your hundredth prayer of the morning could protect them till they pass through towering wooden doors into the safety zone of sacred space enclosed within the cathedral's stone walls, a time of morning not unlike dusk, like the end of this busy, busy day when we arrived in St.-Pierre then promptly lost ourselves in its labyrinth of narrow streets, asking directions to the ruins, finding dead ends, one-ways, a wedding, the chaos of an open market blocks long shutting itself down for the night, climbing higher and higher through cobbled streets like corridors or courtyards or barricaded construction sites and now at last, almost too late to see what we'd set out early that morning and driven many miles to see, parking on top of this steep hill with its commanding view, then unloading ourselves from the car and weaving through a maze of massive, charred stones, the ruins beginning to disappear just at the moment we reach them, blackened stones swallowed by the swiftly dropping (or does it rise) blackness of night, it's about 6:30 and in a couple more minutes only the lights of St.-Pierre would be visible below, outlining the basket-handle-curve *anse* of its waterfront, the marina, docks, fishing wharves, and beaches, the slave dungeon and fort above it bristling with cannon in the middle of the harbor's sweep, illumined like a carnival to lure tourists to shops, souvenir kiosks, snack stalls and restaurants bunched below stone ramparts that rise hundreds of feet to armor the hillside, already dark down there along the waterfront while at this height a bright dusk holds just long enough for us to read plaques fastened to a fragment of wall and learn that the frightened faithful had gathered here nearly a hundred years before, two dozen or so of them the morning of May 8, 1902, to receive communion at the Church of Our Lady, arriving in the morning at about the same hour—six—that we arrived in the evening, the end of their lives coming very shortly when Mount Pelée erupts, the Big Bang after weeks of rumbling and spitting hot ash and drooling floods of boiling mud down its flanks till finally, literally the mountain blew its top, its goddamn mind, its pent-up rage or God's rage or just the inevitable, traumatic climax of eons of tectonic plates shifting and magma sliding, heat and steam and friction and grinding, locked-down pressure exploding, tossing rocks big as barns, as cathedrals, a mile in the air or pulverizing, splintering, expelling solid acres of rock as dust finer than grains of sand, grains of salt, grains of sugar, a pyroclastic surge leveling the city, annihilating the entire population of St.-Pierre, except for two alleged survivors, one a black man named Cyparis, saved because he was confined drunk in a dungeon, the other a white man just extraordinarily lucky, 30,000 killed because St.-Pierre's citizens, for the usual head-in-the-sand reasons and perhaps some not so usual (including a calculated campaign of disinformation organized by politicians who wanted voters to stay put for an imminent election) ignored the volcano's warnings and chose to treat Pelée's palpable menace like a murderous, intriguing neighbor locked safely behind bars, even arranged day-trips to observe the mountain's muted fury and violence and reassure themselves that the danger was far away and contained, perhaps they also believed the abiding ordinariness of their lives, the city's scale would protect them, their faith in God charm away the inconceivable cataclysm of a large, bustling urban center's sudden and total extinction, anyway the inhabitants of St.-Pierre were forewarned emphatically, yet few if any chose to grab their hats and git while the gittin' was good and on the final morning a few of the 30,000 or so hangers-on, according to the memorial plaques in French and English that we struggled to decipher in the waning light, had slunk out of their beds and trudged up winding, cobbled streets, a column of somnambulists, all social classes and colors but uniformly dulled to a faded, bluish gray by the peculiar pallor of that dawn's light, ghostly pilgrims wending their way here to the hilltop where we stand, their shoes if they bothered to wear them or owned shoes or had located shoes in the mess of lives shattered, lives on hold, displaced, dispossessed of the ordinary, shoed or shoeless naked feet coated with the dirty snow clinging to everything now, St.-Pierre in its turn inundated by the dust storms that had covered Le Morne Rouge, Ajoupa- Bouillon, Petit Savan, all the mountain villages that had sent caravans of panicked evacuees to the capital, an unheeded early-warning system through which Mount Pelée announced its evil intentions, emptying towns, frightening away birds or silencing the few too confused to flee, swelling and rerouting rivers, rousting snakes from underground lairs, agitating dogs so they howled all night, and now for a week the city folks' feet shuffling through velvet grit, hands and brooms useless against the *petite neige* raining constantly, producing an odd, blue-white haze, even sunsets had strayed down the spectrum from the usual bold reds, golds, and purples to silver and white, and in the early-morning hours of May 8, 1902, some of the faithful mount the switchback, rough-hewn streets of St.-Pierre to swallow the wafer of flesh, drink the wine of blood, pray for a blessing, for salvation eternal, but first O Merciful God deliver us from the demon volcano howling and thundering, shaking and quivering like a berserk demon whose burning fingers grasp for our children, O Lord, now in the hour of our need, our desperation, stretch forth Thy gentle hand we beseech thee at this darkening hour, a dawn a little like the dusk Katrine and I pick our way through when finally we reach this summit floating above the former capital city, light dropping out of the sky like a shot bird and a gold scrim edging the highest mountain ridges like foam crowning breakers, the last of day sinking fast into last ditch flashes of sea, at this hour reversed or recycled or upside down, 6:00 P.M. to 6:00 A.M., when a century ago a man pauses a moment to oversee the last twenty yards of his weary family's march into God's house and considers, in the fifteen seconds he spares himself to contemplate it, man's fate, the ways of God to man because, after all, after all the work and prayers and sweat and failures and small triumphs and the evil he'd done to others and they to him and disappointments with himself and the island's general calamities he'd survived, its featureless, countless dead lost in cyclones, hurricanes, fires, floods, deadly centuries of slavery and sugarcane cultivation, so many gone, leaving no trace and now the precious few close to him dying off as he ages, the mystery of bad people's good fortune while misfortune dogs the righteous, and on this May morning of the year 1902 the weight of a bizarre, unreasoning, unexpected light so caustic he blinks and tears and gags on the hellfire odor of sulfur, who would have thought that in spite of so much that had truly surprised him about a man's life and so much that had become dully, dreadfully predictable, so much he never would have guessed he'd be able to bear or bear missing, the needful things he'd never attained, the lies and compromises rationalized and once in a great while quiet repose emptying and filling him like an angel's cool, sweet breath, who would have guessed, who could have imagined a man's life could consist exactly, no more, no less, of the things he'd done and beheld, just that and nothing more, only that, and just at the moment he stands, balanced on one leg like a stork, dusting the toe of his boot on the back of his pant leg, not yet ready to enter the vast church where his wife and children are probably kneeling in prayer, he's still wondering how a life can be such a large and little thing, just then is when an earsplitting rumble shakes him as the mountain flexes till its muscles burst, and its flesh flies as hot iron pellets, as missiles of mud and cinder, as a tsunami of chest-collapsing, bone-crushing heat, radiance, and wind to the spot where the man hovers and drop him in his tracks, imprints him like an etching on glass, a blood-dark shadow on one of the granite blocks that once served as a threshold to the cathedral, the hulking stone church, clock tower, and civic center no more a match for Pelée's fury than the man's meat and bone, everything around him collapsing in a tottering, totalizing instant, shattered, squashed, breaking apart in slow motion—if you could watch with eyes moving faster than the speed of light—monumental structures scattering themselves precisely, all the toy parts tumbling down, stately almost, like the fragments of Ozymandias's statue arranging themselves into a rune on the desert sand, Look over there, Katrine, a guy might have been standing in front of the church, over where all those big stone blocks are, on the steps maybe, standing there before he got scorched and splashed, see that slab sticking up, the big one leaning on the pile, maybe a step once, maybe one of the king-size polished granite steps leading to the cathedral's entrance, to the double doors where people exiting the dark interior would be smacked by a stunning, sumptuous view of sky and sea and mountaintops stretching to the horizon, a sight, though the church long gone, Katrine and I are privileged to enjoy, just for a moment or two at the edge of the hilltop, because we took our time driving here, didn't we, baby, a lifetime to reach this grim, rapturous spot, girl, almost too late, didn't we come close to missing altogether these moments together that seem to exhaust themselves too quick, too sweet, my love, to quite believe, night falling and/or rising and we can barely read the signs, the official account of worshipers who were receiving communion (or did it say confirmation) exactly at the instant Pelée erupted, brutally, conclusively interrupting the service, the tenure of cathedral, clock tower, and municipal buildings erected to loom over St.-Pierre forever, these scrambled, jigsaw boulders on the crest of a hill, blackened by fire and heat rays a century ago, huge blocks of stone still cracked, split and spilled, exposed where they tumbled that morning when an entire city sleeping below the church disappeared, too, May 8, 1902, says the plaque, at 6:00 A.M. I think it says, these plaques we try to read in failing light, Katrine, do you remember the skinny, scruffy, typecast ghetto dog watching us, too curious about our business to be just an innocent mutt that happens to stray pit-pat-patter through the stony ruins each evening at this precise hour, the hour of our tardy arrival because we took our time driving up the coast, beginning lazily at our hotel in Ste.-Anne, then through Marin of course, the gateway it seemed to everywhere else we wanted to venture on the island, then the highway N2 or what passes for highway along miles of its length except when the main drag between south and north does its impersonation of a dusty, two-lane, twisting country road, then it's N2 again, a superhighway skirting Rivière-Sallie into Le Lamentin, around the edges of the present capital Fort-de-France, then north to suburban towns such as Bellevue and Schoelcher-by-the-Sea terraced serenely against a mountainside that swoops nearly perpendicular into the sea, more steep hills decorated with sprawling mansions and I bet most, if not all, belong to *békés,* the descendants of old-school gangsters, the original European colonists who emigrated from France, can they see us from their wraparound verandas, our underpowered, underbraked rental car whining on precipitous climbs and shuddering on stark winding descents that treat us to breathtaking, liver-grabbing blind curves, startling vistas spread glistening to the horizon then suddenly disappearing only to pop out again as you cling to a narrow ledge cut into one mountain's shoulder, glide down the sheer drop of another, ogling, oohing and aahing, itching to stop the car and stare, to cool your hot feet in the dazzling sea, sit and watch the chariot race of braces of whitecaps vying to be the first to die on arcs of golden beach scalloped here, there and everywhere from the rocky base of the mountains, motoring into Case-Pilote and Bellefontaine wondering how to absorb and hold onto the show-off landscape's primp and impossible good looks, the supermodel bling-bling runway sashaying of its charms, its forever fashionable sheen of untouchable beauty so abundant, so striking and clarifying and over-the-top that you wonder at the wondrousness and fault yourself for doubting, give up before you start because no account, no words, no pictures, no song you could fabricate would ever do the island justice, even as you feel the urge to do just that, to somehow digest and internalize and spit out in some transmittable, preservable form what you're seeing because it's too much, you need to share it or it will bust you open, or worse, desert you and you'll be empty-handed, devastated, you need someone to smile or wag his or her head and testify, yes, amen, convince you with their witness the wondrousness is real, that it was and is and will last, this free-fall cavorting in a tin-can automobile along the serpentine shore, roller-coasting ups and downs and switchbacks and narrow escapes when the road shrinks to one head-on skimpy lane and you're sure you're going to ram another car between Bellefontaine and Le Carbet, lose it all, disintegrating in a fiery, histrionic crash, down, down a sheer cliffside when an oncoming Renault, Peugeot, or Citroën bumps you off the road, down, down, skidding, flopping, exploding on this road to St.-Pierre where many villagers risked body and soul flying fast as feet or horse or mule or cart could carry them, away from the volcano's boiling maw, the galloping Earth in pursuit, a pitiless, bubbling lake of fiery mud spreading faster than chickens or pigs or goats can scurry out of its path, blind runaways careering down dangerous mountain trails in spite of enveloping darkness relieved only by Pelée's smoldering, flame-licked peak yes yes you could leap suddenly to your death off this skimpy road but the alternative more horrible still, the slowly encroaching doom of the bored mud's scalding, smothering ooze catching you asleep in your bed, so you drive at a breakneck pace, twisting, turning, peeling rubber when there's open road, pedal to the metal till Katrine asks what's the hurry and, after all, there is none and she's uncomfortable with such unnecessary speed and when I slow down enough to think about it, damn, so am I, and from that point on we continue our tour more moderately, no less wary of what's behind us waiting its evil chance to pounce if we take too deep a breath, but our rhythm changes, the day expands, extends itself as we stop at the Gauguin Museum just beyond Le Carbet, see relics of the incinerated city, bizarre St.-Pierre artifacts of glass, ceramics, metal reheated, reshaped as in Pompeii meltdowns, see copies of twelve paintings the master completed while he recuperated here in 1886 on the way to the rest of his art, to Paris, the islands of France *outre-mer,* the Museum of Modern Art in New York City, Gauguin drawn like so many European wanderers before him to distant regions of the Earth, legions of culturally deprived, restless white male explorers, exploiters, adventurers seeking places, as Gauguin noted in a letter to his mom, where *the blood isn't spoiled yet* (whose?), Gauguin sailing to Martinique from Panama after sunstroke, mosquitoes, and coolie, nigger, wog, spic labor digging a ditch across the isthmus nearly killed him and his companion, finds here on this green isle a respite, a healing paradise in comparison to the Canal Zone's misery, encountering, in addition to the patronizing *békés,* a brown, sturdy people who welcome and instruct him, whose Creole skin, clothes, motion, and voices inform his sense of color, of rhythm, teach him new connections between light and dark, love and melancholy, work and play, life and death, teach lightness of spirit and depth of shadow until he sails away, healthy again, questing further, carrying memories of flesh tones, textures, and patterns he'll look for again and rediscover again in Tahiti, Gauguin revealing on canvas the tropical island of his heart, or rather what he wishes to find in that desiccated, encrusted space if ever the scales of Europe are removed from it, a naked heart, Europe naked loving, embracing the image of itself the painter dreams, the heat this island schooled him to reclaim, to search and plunder mercilessly and then after the Gauguin Museum we stop at Habitation Anse Latouche nestled among abrupt hills slamming down into the sea, Martinique's *plus belle grande case,* just what Monsieur Dorange ordered and had built in 1643, offering the mansion as part of his daughter's dowry to Monsieur François Le Vassor who later was ennobled as DeLatouche, thus the handle Habitation Latouche for this spectacularly profitable site of sugar plantation, indigo dying vats, a manioc factory, rum distillery powered by both hydraulic and steam-driven wheels, an elaborate system of elevated aqueducts, a vast, sulky posse of African slaves, fieldworkers who cultivate, cut, haul, and crush the cane, baptizing the land with their blood and sweat, African artisans and mechanics who built whatever the plantation required, African engineers, agronomists, wizards, musicians, whores, chroniclers, philosophers, mothers, scholars, drunks, cooks, runaways, saints, renegades, all colors, genders, ages, sizes invested here, imprisoned here, buried here, in this grave-quiet Habitation Latouche, Africans whose muteness, tonguelessness overcomes me, sits me down on a stone bench and keeps me sitting still,

still so I can listen, interrogate the silence with my own, attend the muted spirits, summon them, beg them to forgive me for appalling distance, appalling ignorance, forgive me for not avenging their terror, their captivity, their immolation in *béké* ovens whose fires they tended and fed with the fuel of their own dark bodies, my body, my lost brethren I summon you, beg you to summon me, when our time comes, time to smash and efface, to rest, to find peace, to forgive, Katrine and I the only visitors for the hour or so we spend exploring this lush, intricate killing ground, its rusting machines, its vegetation, its stone ruins, the pervasive melancholy silence of mourning unbroken except for our whispers (whispering, we agree without saying so, the only permissible register for our voices here), thick, thick silence until a sudden onslaught of howling startles us as I was startled from sleep our first morning on the island by unearthly squeals outside the room in Ste.-Anne's Belfond resort, 436 Bequia, that eerie predawn intrusion repeating itself this afternoon in Habitation Latouche and I haven't pinned down the source yet in either place, maybe the pale, horned zebu cattle tormented by mosquitoes, someone suggested, or the unquiet souls of those kidnaped and raped and tortured and worked to death on the island, who knows except the sound both times reminded me of peacocks shrieking in the garden of the Swan Tavern back in my Rhodes Scholar days at Oxford University in England, a bunch of us crossing the commons, green, muddy fields at one edge of town, home to gaggles of strutting geese, flights of pheasants that would wheel up, alarmed by the loud suck of our soggy footsteps, the heads of my companions—fellow Americans, presumably the best and brightest young men of our generation, at Oxford to be groomed for the civilizing mission a bandit named Cecil Rhodes called "the world's fight"—haloed by the stubborn light that hangs in northern skies even after sunset, on our way to a turf- and dung-smelling riverside pub with its scraggly, rainbow-tailed captive birds, their unnerving yowls somehow fitting as black pints of Guinness at dusk on those midsummer eves, Habitation Latouche an early outpost of the mission, the burden we Rhodes scholars had been anointed to assume, the white man's burden I'd been schooled to believe mine too, spreading the net of civilization to green islands such as Martinique, sparkling as England sparkles in its emerald seas, the Latouche plantation, too, ensconced in an ocean of greenery, a fertile, well-watered vale that framed the big house, one slope above *la grande case* dotted with stone slave kennels folded discreetly out of sight, unless you're looking for them, low huts spared by a cyclone that wiped most of the big house off the face of the Earth, leaving behind a few Gothic-arched, two-story sections of stone outer wall to signify the grandeur of a mansion designed to be airy and luminous, the brochure says, pierced by numerous rows of windows and protected from the heat by balustrades and galleries, by groves of trees whose ancient canopies now shade a blazing patchwork of tropical flowers and blossoming shrubs, the remnants of fountains, gazebos, an arcade of statueless pedestals, stone paths sprouting grass through split seams, crumbled retaining walls partitioning emptiness and desolation, all surrounded by green, so much green, so many greens layered and Edens layered here under a vast blue sky, and I recall noticing a restaurant's backyard through the trees at the foot of the hill where the plantation merges with jungle and wonder if peacocks might be kept there, and on our way out query the pretty beige girl at the Habitation ticket and information counter but she doesn't understand my question because I don't know the French word for peacock and for some reason Katrine, reliable keeper of a remarkable hoard of words in two languages, can't remember either so we left behind the silence, left behind as if they never happened the mysterious bawling, tortured screams and leisurely drove to our next stop, the sea, a stretch of beach just beyond a little stone bridge that arched gracefully over the road, a brackish-smelling, gray-sand beach crowded with European tourists and a sprinkling of darker locals, a beach abutting the roadway, lined for half a mile or so by a flock of the ubiquitous mammy wagons that vend drinks and grilled chicken, *beignets, accras,* fritters of conch and cod, crepes stuffed with everything from chocolate to guava jelly to cheese to shrimp, and parking next to one of these cornucopias, we disembark and order a snack from a big black lady who frowned five minutes before she grinned once beneath the paisley kerchief tied Aunt Jemima-style around her head or did we order later, after we hit the water, or to be more precise, after Katrine swam and I just wet my toes because the steep incline of the beach made underwater footing treacherous, at least from the perspective of a wobbly, chicken-hearted nonswimmer who will brave breaking waves up to his chin if there's a hard, level floor of sand under his toes but if I can't tell where my next underwater step might take me I'd prefer to watch and so I did, stretched out on a towel in a pool of some of the last sun hitting the beach that particular day, just beyond the edge of a shadow cast by a boulder-heaped thrust of land jutting from the sea, a hillside that framed the near end of the beach, my view otherwise unimpeded so bright sea shimmers in front of me out to the horizon where the sun poised like a molten wafer judiciously measures the distance between itself and the water's salty lips and to my left if I shade my eyes and squint I could watch Katrine swimming, her hands white gloves exploding with each stroke, she's parallel to the shore now and I imagine the ritual I'd missed, so familiar I didn't need to see it to see her acclimating herself to the water, how she hesitates, delaying the plunge, making faces, slapping, fussing at the waves, vaulting straight up when her back's splashed, protesting, as if she'd rather be anyplace in the universe than here fighting the water's chilly for a minute grip but convincing no one, certainly not herself, green eyes sparkling, skin gemmed with beauty grains of glistening sea, then she's off, there she goes and the wave she chooses breaks foaming white over her head and I think of the waters inside and outside her, the panicky instant when the vastness of one threatens the minuscule droplet of the other, how would she, how does she, how long could anyone survive the humongous onslaught, the last thing seen the pale soles of her feet, two bunches of toes sucked under, kicking, digging into the unfurling wave and think of how water and women have been linked in my life, how my understanding of women has been tempered and flawed by watery metaphors, liquid intuitions certainly all wet and very confused at times, how once I believed I required, even deserved by some sort of male divine right, a woman no other man had touched, my own private fish from the fishy

fishy sea and wondered when I met someone new and attractive if some other guy or guys might have been there first and if she'd fallen hook line and sinker before I had my chance and then I would despair at the cruel thought of being anyone besides the first and only one in the deepest heartfelt heart (and pussy, of course) of whatever woman fate would doom me to love forever and ever and now, watching Katrine swim, I realize I haven't quite shed such embarrassingly macho expectations, preoccupations, and double standards, think the hurting thought of other men entering her, remember how surprised I was when she said it works both ways, you know, I think of you in bed with other women and it doesn't make me happy either, she said, and I think how each encounter, each penetration and mixing is like her taut, mermaid's body entering the water at beach after beach as we coast along, touring the shores of this island, the many seas and one surrounding, washing the land, waters constantly changing, waters exchanged, never the same water twice, always more, a different pleasure, for a different woman swimming in a different sea each time, Katrine in her blue- and white-spotted bikini or just the bottom of it or the two of us playing naked in the shallows some glorious mornings at Pointe-Ste.-Marie opposite the Devil's Table, and I think of Yeats's mackerel-crowded seas, salmon spawning, rivers lush with sperm and for a moment I'm free from the need to possess, as if I ever could or should possess Katrine's fiery otherness—free to stop asking myself *who was she* or *who was I* each time we had let go and dived into pleasure or plunged into love with another, and I think how it ain't nothing but a party, after all, and encounters with another's body may prove anything or everything or nothing beyond how doggedly, fiercely, hungrily the dance goes on, chemicals, molecules, bodies attracted to mingle, replenish themselves, the salty brews within and without nearly identical yet also profoundly separate, joining, clashing, sucking, swallowing, braiding, pulling away and joining again, in synch, at risk, at play, watch Katrine clamber out of the smashing, grinding waves, her dash to a towel, collapsing on it, laughing, shivering, shutting her eyes, then baking in the sun, what's within and without balanced, poised, at peace together, each encounter a universe created and erased by its own laws, each meeting fragile as the medium that is source and substance of creatures who must die to be born, who become enraptured by the flow of accident, who are at the mercy of precarious combinations and permutations like those producing once and only once for instance, the two of us, here, alive at dusk in St.-Pierre wading through the blackened stones of a vanished cathedral at the end of a day so fine and exhilarating I'm suddenly self-conscious, overwhelmed almost by the need not to possess but to share the plenitude, share my fullness because there's so much, too much to squander or hoard just for myself, just for a day, so I want to share, I'm brimming with the story of the day, the pleasure and need to tell it, then nervous because I might screw it up, might leave out something real or intrude something fake and spoil it or might not remember to invent something when invention would render more life or might forget to prune facts when facts detract from vitality, and I hope the scowling, sneaky dog we saw earlier patrolling the borders of this hilltop plot of ruins is not a cop dog, not a cyborg snitch because it catches my lady squatting between a couple of refrigerator-size stones tinkling into the grass what she can't contain a second longer and it catches me loosing a steaming Mount Pelée burst, huddled in my pocket of shadow, and if the mutt's that kind of skulking, officious mutt it will surely trot to the authorities and tattle on us, accuse us of desecrating holy ground.

ABOUT THE AUTHOR

John Edgar Wideman is the only author to have won the PEN/Faulkner Award twice—for the novel *Sent for You Yesterday* in 1984, and for *Philadelphia Fire* in 1990. He is the recipient of numerous other awards, including the American Book Award, the MacArthur Award, and a Lannan Literary Fellowship. His latest book, the acclaimed memoir *Hoop Roots,* was published in 2001.

This book is set in Garamond 3, designed by Morris Fuller Benton and Thomas Maitland Cleland in the 1930s, and Monotype Grotesque, both released digitally by Adobe.

Printed by R. R. Donnelley and Sons on Gladfelter 60-pound Thor Offset smooth white antique paper.

Dust jacket printed by Miken Companies. Color separation by Quad Graphics.

Three-piece case of Ecological Fiber side panels with Sierra black book cloth as the spine fabric. Stamped in Lustrofoil metallic silver.

OTHER TITLES IN THE SERIES

JAN MORRIS *A Writer's House in Wales*
OLIVER SACKS *Oaxaca Journal*
W. S. MERWIN *The Mays of Ventadorn*
WILLIAM KITTREDGE *Southwestern Homelands*
DAVID MAMET *South of the Northeast Kingdom*
GARRY WILLS *Mr. Jefferson's University*
A. M. HOMES *Los Angeles: People, Places, and the Castle on the Hill*

UPCOMING AUTHORS

FRANCINE PROSE *on Sicily*
LOUISE ERDRICH *on Ontario*
PETER CAREY *on Japan*
ARIEL DORFMAN *on Northern Chile*
JAMAICA KINCAID *on Nepal*
ROBERT HUGHES *on Barcelona*
SUSANNA MOORE *on Kauai*
KATHRYN HARRISON *on Santiago de Compostela*
ANNA QUINDLEN *on London*
HOWARD NORMAN *on Nova Scotia*
BARRY UNSWORTH *on Crete*
GEOFFREY WOLFF *on Maine*
PAUL WATKINS *on Norway*
JON LEE ANDERSON *on Andalucia*
DIANE JOHNSON *on Paris*
WILLIAM LEAST HEAT-MOON *on Western Ireland*

NATIONAL GEOGRAPHIC DIRECTIONS

Featuring works by some of the world's most prominent and highly regarded literary figures, National Geographic Directions captures the spirit of travel and of place for which National Geographic is renowned, bringing fresh perspective and renewed excitement to the art of travel writing.